A Salute to
COOKING

Ode to the Soldier Cook

From West Berlin to Hong Kong
From Cyprus to Belize
One soldier always will appear
In heat wave and in freeze.

He may be old, he may be young,
He may be fat or skinny.
The lads all laugh as he goes by,
The soldier in his pinny.

He's just the bloke who burns the toast,
Who moans the least and does the most,
Who rises to the cockerels call,
And leaves the camp behind them all.

He feeds the lads on exercise,
From breakfast through to tea
He feeds the chaps in messes too,
So versatile is he.

29th Field Kitchen © 2009

A Salute to
COOKING

CELEBRITY RECIPES IN AID OF
THE CHELSEA PENSIONERS

Foreword by HRH The Prince of Wales

Compiled by Angela Currie

Bene Factum Publishing

Salute to Cooking
Celebrity Recipes in aid of the Royal Hospital Chelsea
First published in 2009
by Bene Factum Publishing Ltd
PO Box 58122
London
SW8 5WZ

Email: inquiries@bene-factum.co.uk
www.bene-factum.co.uk

ISBN: 978-1-903071-25-0

Every effort has been made to ensure that recipes in this book are the contributor's own work and that we have obtained the appropriate permissions.

A CIP catalogue record of this is available from the British Library

Design and Typesetting by Ian Hughes – Mousemat Design Limited
Printed and bound by Butler Tanner & Dennis Ltd

Cover illustration by Gerald Scarfe CBE

Mixed Sources
Product group from well-managed
forests and other controlled sources
www.fsc.org Cert no. SGS-COC-005091
© 1996 Forest Stewardship Council
FSC

Contents

Acknowledgements

The Chelsea Pensioners' Appeal and Bene Factum Publishing would like to thank the following, whose support has helped to make this book happen:

The Worshipful Company of Cooks

Smith & Williamson

Peter Jones – The John Lewis Partnership

The Worshipful Company of Grocers

Geronimo Inns – The Phoenix

 British Forces Broadcasting Services – www.bfbs.com
DAB Digital Radio

 3663 First for Foodservice – leading foodservice delivered wholesaler (www.3663.co.uk)

Photographs on pages 17, 19, 29, 45, 65, 67, 75, 81, 97, 101, 109, 119, 127, 129, 145, 147, 161, 173, 191, 193, 195, 203, 207 courtesy of www.Fabfoodpix.com

Royal Hospital Chelsea images by Nick Panagakis *Photography*

Introduction

In 1860 Mrs Isabella Beeton wrote, *'I must frankly own, that if I had known, beforehand, that this book would have cost me the labour which it has, I should never have been courageous enough to commence it.'* I know exactly how she felt.

This compilation of favourite recipes from well-known people from all walks of life has been a labour of love: love for the Chelsea Pensioners, among whom I have had the privilege of living for the past 4 years. They did their bit for our country, and I felt it was my turn to do something for them.

Over two years ago I began to raise funds to cover the cost of producing this book, so that all profit from sales would go directly to the Chelsea Pensioners' Appeal, the purpose of which is to modernise their antiquated accommodation which, were he to return today, Wren would still recognise.

I am indebted to those who have generously sponsored the book, those who have contributed recipes, Gerald Scarfe for drawing the wonderful cover and several others who have helped with the project. But above all I want to thank the publisher Anthony Weldon, of Bene Factum Publishing, who has given exceptionally generously of his time and advice. Without him this idea would never have taken flight.

My thanks also go to: Mark Armstrong, Denis Barnham, Stephen Cooper, David Hellens, Heather Holden Brown, Janice Hughes, Major Harry Lomas MBE BEM, Sir Idris Pearce, Lady Walker, Samantha Wyndham; and especially my husband for his forbearance.

Thank you for buying this book. In doing so you are supporting a splendid cause: and I am sure you will enjoy trying out the eclectic selection of recipes it contains.

Angela Currie

CLARENCE HOUSE

As Patron of the Chelsea Pensioners' Appeal, it gives me the greatest pleasure to introduce "A Salute to Cooking". This book has been produced to raise funds for the Royal Hospital's development programme and the impressive list of those who have contributed their favourite recipes speaks volumes for the affection in which the Nation holds the Chelsea Pensioners - and rightly so.

Founded in 1682, "for the succour and relief of veterans broken by age and war", the Royal Hospital has, for well over 300 years, provided a home to successive generations of old and infirm soldiers to whom we all owe an enormous debt of gratitude. If this is to continue, then it is essential that the accommodation is made fit for purpose in the 21st Century. After my recent visit to open the new Infirmary, it is wonderful to see how sympathetic the new accommodation is to the spirit of the place.

I do hope you enjoy trying some of these recipes, and I am sure you will savour them even more in the knowledge that, by buying a copy of this book, you have made your own contribution to the future of this most important National Institution.

Publisher's Note

The very nature of this book is that it is made up of generous personal contributions. These recipes came to us in many different formats. We have tried to standardise them so that there is some uniformity throughout the book and they are easy to follow. At the same time we have been careful not to lose the individuality of the original recipes.

This has meant that elements can vary from recipe to recipe – the most obvious example being as to how many people the recipe is for. Also, in some cases the instructions are a bit general, and the quantities a little imprecise – under these circumstances please use your judgement as you best think fit, and to suit your individual tastes.

Oven Temperatures

Centigrade	Farenheit	Gas Mark	Verbal
100°	225°	¼	Very slow/Very low
120°	250°	½	Very slow/Very low
140°	275°	1	Slow/Low
150°	300°	2	Slow/Low
160°	325°	3	Moderately slow/Warm
180°	350°	4	Moderate/Medium
190°	375°	5	Moderate/Moderately hot
200°	400°	6	Moderately hot
220°	425°	7	Hot
230°	450°	8	Hot/Very hot
250°	475°	9	Very hot
260°	500°	10	Extremely hot

Weights

Imperial	Metric	Imperial	Metric
¼ oz	5 g	7½ oz	210 g
½ oz	10 g	8 oz	225 g
¾ oz	20 g	8½ oz	235 g
1 oz	25 g	9 oz	250 g
1½ oz	40 g	9½ oz	260 g
2 oz	50 g	10 oz	275 g
2½ oz	60 g	10½ oz	285 g
3 oz	75 g	11 oz	310 g
3½ oz	85 g	12 oz	350 g
4 oz	110 g	1 lb	450 g
4½ oz	125 g	1 lb 2 oz	500 g
5 oz	150 g	2 lb	900 g
5½ oz	160 g	2½ lb	1.1 kg
6 oz	175 g	3 lb	1.3 kg
6½ oz	185 g	3½ lb	1.6 kg
7 oz	200 g	4 lb	2 kg

Volume

Cups	Imperial/fl oz	Imperial/pint	Metric
	1 fl oz		28 ml
	4 fl oz		112 ml
½ cup	5 fl oz	¼ pint	142 ml
1 cup	8.45 fl oz	0.43 pint	250 ml
	10 fl oz	½ pint	284 ml
	10.10 fl oz	0.52 pint	300 ml
	15 fl oz	¾ pint	426 ml
2 cups	16 fl oz	0.83 pint	473 ml
	20 fl oz	1 pint	568 ml
4 cups	32 fl oz	1.7 pints	946 ml
	35 fl oz		1 litre
	40 fl oz	2 pints	1.13 litres
	70 fl oz	3.5 pints	2 litres

A Wartime Victory Menu
Marguerite Patten OBE
CHEF AND HOME ECONOMIST

This is typical of a meal which would be served for VE or VJ days in 1945. At that time I was one of the many Food Advisers, working for the Ministry of Food. Our job was to give the maximum of help about food to all in Britain. I describe us as being 'the front line troops' for the Ministry.

I was fortunate enough to be among the crowds outside Buckingham Palace to celebrate VE Day. How we cheered, danced and embraced complete strangers on that wonderful evening. There was a joy in travelling home without any fear of air raid warnings.

Summer Beetroot Soup

Serve this excellent summertime soup hot or cold

1 pint (600ml) water
4 small or 2 medium cooked beetroot, skinned and coarsely grated
4 medium tomatoes, skinned and finely diced
4 tablespoons chopped spring onions
2 tablespoons chopped parsley
Salt and pepper

Bring the water to the boil, add the ingredients and cook gently for 10 minutes. Serve hot or allow the soup to become cold and well-chilled then serve.

Variation:
Use the same recipe in wintertime but substitute a large finely chopped onion for the spring onions. Simmer this in the water for 10–15 minutes then add the beetroot and about 8 oz (225g) bottled tomato purée and continue as in the recipe above. Omit the fresh tomatoes.

SERVES 4

Cold Meat Pasties

This recipe comes from a wartime book published by McDougalls. This high amount of Worcestershire Sauce, which may be reduced, is typical of recipes of the era, as people tried to put as much flavour as possible into fairly flavourless food.

Shortcrust Pastry:
8 oz (225g) flour
Pinch of salt
4 oz (110g) fat – margarine and lard mixed or cooking fat
   or good dripping
Cold water to bind

For the filling:
8 oz (225g) cold meat, minced
1 small onion, minced or chopped
2 tomatoes, sliced
2 tablespoons chopped cooked carrots or other vegetables
2 tablespoons Worcestershire Sauce
2 tablespoons gravy or water
Salt and pepper
1 reconstituted dried egg or fresh egg, if available, to glaze

1. Preheat the oven to 200C/400F/Gas mark 6. Grease a baking tray.
2. Sift the flour and salt into a mixing bowl. Rub in the fat until the mixture is like fine breadcrumbs. Add sufficient water to make a dough with a firm rolling consistency.
3. Roll out the pastry and cut it into four rounds. Brush the edges with water or a little beaten egg. Mix the ingredients for the filling together and put in the centre of each round. Bring the edges together, pinch well and trim into flutes between the finger and thumb.
4. Make a slit in the side of the pastry with a pointed knife. Brush with beaten egg, if liked. Place on the baking tray and bake in the preheated oven for 20 minutes.

Vegetable Pasties
Follow the recipe for Cold Meat Pasties above, but fill the pastry with about 1 lb (450g) lightly cooked diced vegetables, such as onions, carrots, turnips, potatoes and swede, 1–2 chopped uncooked tomatoes give extra flavour. Use less Worcestershire Sauce and a little tomato ketchup to flavour.

MAKES 4 PASTIES

Fruit Crisp

1 lb (450g) fruit, weighed when prepared i.e. peeled or stoned
2–3 tablespoons water (see method)
1 oz (25g) sugar

For the topping:
1 oz (25g) margarine or cooking fat
1 oz (25g) sugar
1 tablespoon golden syrup
4 oz (100g) rolled oats

1. Preheat the oven to 180C/350F/Gas mark 5. Grease a 1½ pint (900ml) pie dish. Put the fruit into the pie dish with the water and 1 oz (25g) sugar. If using ripe soft fruit, use only about 1 tablespoon water. Cover the pie dish and bake firm fruits for 10–15 minutes and soft fruits for 5–10 minutes.
2. Put the margarine or cooking fat into a saucepan, add the sugar and syrup. Stir over a low heat until the ingredients have melted.
3. Remove from the heat and stir in the rolled oats. Blend thoroughly then spread over the fruit in a flat layer.
4. Bake in the preheated oven for 30 minutes or until the topping is golden brown. Serve hot or cold.

SERVES 4

Feeding the Nation by Marguerite Patten (Hamlyn 2005) Copyright © Marguerite Patten 2005

Starters

. . . to start the day
Breakfast Smoothie

Pumpkin, Honey and Sage Soup
Zucchini Ripieni – Stuffed Courgettes
Guacamole
Vegetable and Chervil Soup 'Facon Maman Blanc'
Crab Florentine
Smoked Mackerel Paté
Watercress Soup
Prawns in Tomato Aspic
Pea and Ham Soup
Vegetable Soup
Chilled Consommé and Avocado
Stolen Fish Chowder
Watermelon, Feta and Black Olive Salad
Chicken and Sweetcorn Soup
London Particular
Narial (Coconut), Tomato and Crab Shorba (Soup)
Roasted Tomato Soup with a Purée of Basil
Gazpacho
Proper Tomato Soup
Pea Cappuccino

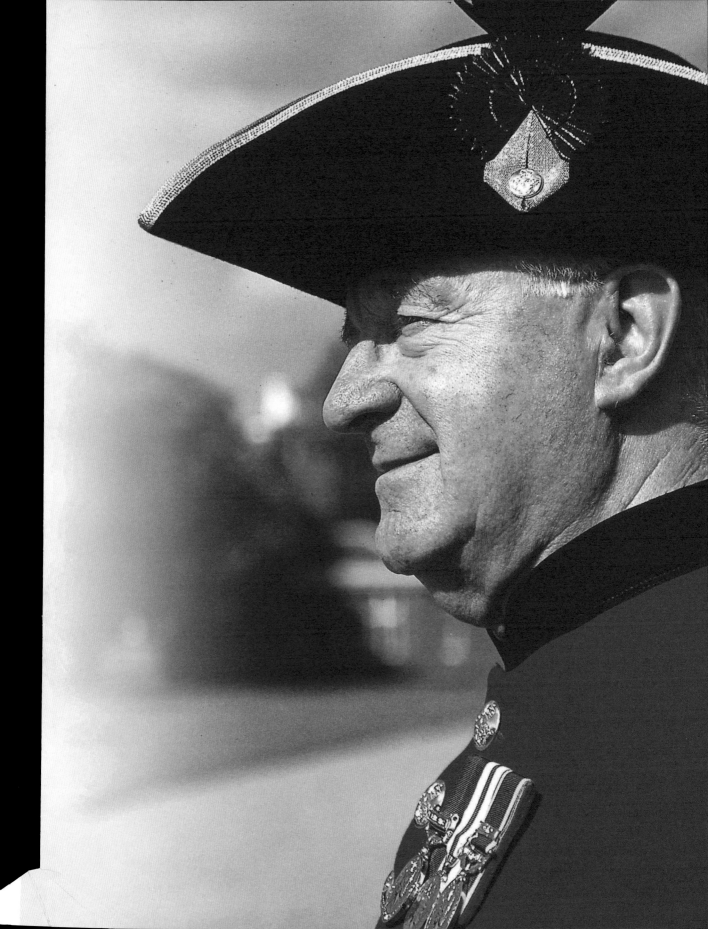

Sir Stuart Hampson

CHAIRMAN JOHN LEWIS PARTNERSHIP 1993–2007

Breakfast Smoothie

I always started my working day with this smoothie when I was Chairman of the John Lewis Partnership.

> 1 banana, roughly sliced
> 1 small pot of fruit yoghurt
> 1 tablespoon of wheatmeal
> 2 tablespoons of oatmeal
> 1 cup of milk
>
> Put all the ingredients into a liquidiser, blend until smooth and start the day!

'Never work before breakfast; if you have to work before breakfast, eat your breakfast first.'
Josh Billings

Tom Aikens
CHEF AND RESTAURATEUR

Pumpkin, Honey and Sage Soup

1kg pumpkin, peeled and cut into 1 cm cubes
6g fresh sage, finely chopped
80g unsalted butter
15g sea salt
85g honey
130g double cream
1 litre chicken stock
15g lemon juice

1. Heat a pan on a low heat then add the butter so it just melts
(not brown).
2. Add the squash along with the sage, sea salt, honey and
lemon juice. Cover with a lid so the vegetables sweat and cook
for 10 minutes on the low heat.
3. Stir the vegetables now and again so they don't brown. Then add
the stock and cream, turn the heat up to full and bring the soup to
a slow boil and then turn the heat down to a simmer for 5 minutes.
4. Turn off the heat and ladle the soup into the blender jug in
2 batches. Only fill it ½ full, then blend the soup for 2–3 minutes
to a fine purée.

SERVES 4

'I live on good soup, not on
fine words.'
Moliere

Mark Armstrong

ENTERTAINMENT ENTREPRENEUR

Zucchini Ripieni – Stuffed Courgettes

This is a very sexy antipasto, popular with kids as well, since it can be eaten with the fingers. Although the recipe originates from the foot of the Piedmont Hills in Biella, North Italy, the dish is popular along the whole Mediterranean Coast – from the chic Cote d'Azure to the cool Amalfi Coast – a real Dolce Vita Delight.

6 large courgettes
50g mortadella or cooked ham, finely chopped
2 eggs
3 big spoons of grated Parmesan
Chopped parsley
Salt and pepper to taste

Béchamel sauce:
2 lumps of butter the size of walnuts
500ml milk
2 large tablespoons of flour
4 tablespoons of Parmesan
A pinch of nutmeg
Salt and pepper to taste

1. Make the béchamel sauce by melting the butter slowly, add the flour and stir with a wooden spoon to make a paste. Slowly add the milk, stirring continuously, then the Parmesan, nutmeg, and salt and pepper as the mixture thickens. It must be thick and have no lumps. Leave to cool.
2. Cook the courgettes in boiling water for 10–15 minutes. Cut them in half lengthwise, scoop out the insides and put in a bowl. Keep the empty shells.
3. To the bowl add the eggs, mortadella, Parmesan, parsley and béchamel sauce. Season and stir until smooth.
4. Fill the courgette shells with the mixture, dot butter on the top and cook for 30 minutes in the oven at 180C/350F/Gas mark 4.
5. When they look crispy and brown on the top take them out and leave them to cool. They are delicious hot or cold and would even reheat – mmmm!

SERVES 4

Dame Eileen Atkins DBE
ACTRESS

Guacamole

I simply love guacamole and this is the best recipe for it, given to me by that great actor Vincent Price. As well as being an amusing man, Vincent was a gourmet and a great cook. I always serve this, as he suggested, in a huge glop on top of shredded lettuce.

2 avocado pears
3 tbsp lemon juice
1 small grated onion
1 small green chilli, finely chopped
⅛ tsp ground coriander
½ clove of garlic, mashed
3 tbsp mayonnaise
3 small tomatoes, peeled, seeded and chopped
Dash of cayenne or Tabasco
Salt

1. Peel and seed the avocados but make sure that you save the seeds.
2. Mash the flesh until it is either smooth or slightly lumpy. I prefer lumpy.
3. Add the rest of the ingredients, mix well, then put the seeds on top. This prevents discolouration.
4. Chill but remove the seeds a little time before serving.
5. Serve before dinner with drinks, crisps or biscuits.

'Part of the secret of success in life is to eat what you like and let the food fight it out inside.'
Mark Twain

Raymond Blanc OBE
CHEF AND RESTAURATEUR

Vegetable and Chervil Soup 'Facon Maman Blanc'

A small tribute to 'Maman Blanc' and, I should say, to 'Papa Blanc' too as most of the vegetables would come from his garden. This soup offers a multitude of flavours varying with the seasons. The choice of vegetables and herbs is completely yours. Chervil is one of my favourite herbs, it is very popular in French cuisine yet is little known and little used in Great Britain. You can also blend the soup for that delightful texture – a spoon of crème fraiche would always be welcome.

15g/1 tbsp butter, unsalted
120g/1 onion, medium finely chopped
5g/1 garlic clove, finely chopped
160g/2 carrots large, finely sliced
300g/2 leeks, medium, outer leaves removed, sliced 1cm
    and washed
3 celery sticks, sliced ½ cm
8g/8 pinches of salt
1g/2 pinches pepper, white freshly ground
1 litre water
1 courgette large, cut in half lengthways and sliced ½ cm
2 tomatoes, ripe, cut in quarters and roughly chopped
15g/1 tbsp butter, unsalted (or sour cream)
25g/1 handful chervil, finely chopped

1. On medium heat sweat the onion, garlic, carrots, celery and leeks in the butter for 5 minutes (no colour) to extract maximum flavour. Season with salt and freshly ground white pepper.
2. Add the boiling water, courgette and tomato (the boiling water will reduce the cooking time and also keep the lively colours). Fast boil for a further 5 minutes. Whisk in the butter (or sour cream or both!) and add the chervil. Taste and correct the seasoning if required.
Pour into a large tureen and serve to your guests.

SERVES 4–6

Photograph Jean Cazals

Chef's tip:
The key to this soup is its fresh, clean flavour. It is critical that you do not muddy the wonderful flavours of your vegetables by over cooking. Just a few minutes will do.

Variations:
This is just the start of a wonderful soup. You could omit the sour cream and chervil and add pesto for a delicious pistou soup. Cooking the soup with a teaspoon of green curry paste, coconut milk, lemon grass, lime leaves, chilli and galangal would produce a delicious soup with flavours from Thailand.

Sir David Brewer CMG JP

HER MAJESTY'S LORD-LIEUTENANT OF GREATER LONDON

Crab Florentine

In order to have a link with my home county, Cornwall, I asked Rick Stein to create a recipe for my Lord Mayor's Banquet in Guildhall in November 2005, and this is it.

25g unsalted butter
400g spinach, picked and washed
500g fresh picked crab meat
450ml milk
1 small onion, studded with cloves
1 bay leaf
6 black peppercorns

Béchamel Sauce
30g butter
30g flour
2 tbsp double cream
75g Parmesan, grated
1 egg yolk
1 sprig of chervil

1. Melt the unsalted butter in a heavy-bottomed pan. Add all the spinach and toss until wilted, drain in a colander and cool.
2. Make a bed of spinach in 6 china dishes then top each dish with a pile of crab meat.
3. Infuse the milk with the onion, bay leaf and peppercorns.
4. Melt the butter in a pan. Add the flour and cook for 1 minute, then whisk in the infused milk to form a sauce.
5. Stir in the cream and Parmesan then cook for a further 5 minutes on a low heat.
6. Remove from the heat, whisk in the egg yolk and check the seasoning.
7. Spoon the sauce over the crab and spinach and grill for 5 minutes until golden brown.
8. Garnish with chervil and serve immediately.

SERVES 6

Rt. Hon. David Cameron MP
POLITICIAN

Smoked Mackerel Paté

This will feed eight greedy people. It is incredibly simple and needs no machinery (or expertise).

> 4 smoked mackerel fillets
> 500 grams of cottage cheese and an equivalent amount
>   of Greek yoghurt
> Juice from 1 lemon
> Freshly milled black pepper
> A teaspoon of strong horseradish sauce
> A few drops of Tabasco

1. Peel the skin off the mackerel fillets and put them in a bowl.
2. Shred them using two forks.
3. Mix in all the other ingredients, stirring vigorously with a fork.
4. Add pepper to taste.
5. Put in the fridge and then serve on toast.

**'An empty stomach is not a
good political advisor.'**
Albert Einstein

25

Rt. Hon. Kenneth Clarke QC MP
POLITICIAN

From: The Rt. Hon. Kenneth Clarke, QC, MP

HOUSE OF COMMONS
LONDON SW1A 0AA

Watercress Soup
(WITH MORE THAN A LITTLE HELP FROM GILLIAN CLARKE!)

2 or 3 bunches of watercress (or 3 supermarket packs)
1½ oz of butter
3 large potatoes (diced)
Chicken stock (a cube will do, or home made stock if you have it)
Milk or cream to taste

1. Soften watercress in butter over a low heat.
2. Add diced potatoes. Stir and cook for a few minutes.
3. Add stock to reach top of vegetables.
4. Simmer until potato is soft.
5. Liquidise and add milk or cream as desired.
6. Reheat gently and serve.

This is a winter version.
For a summer version add less potato and more watercress, in proportion.

Also works well with rocket.

SERVES 6

Major General Peter Currie CB
LIEUTENANT GOVERNOR ROYAL HOSPITAL CHELSEA

Prawns in Tomato Aspic

This is an old favourite: easy to make, and delicious to eat.

1 packet lemon jelly
16 fl oz tomato juice
1 tbsp lemon juice (we like a little more)
Worcestershire Sauce, to taste
6 oz prawns
½ cup celery, finely chopped
1 tbsp stuffed olives, sliced
1 tbsp green pepper, finely chopped
1 tbsp chopped spring onion
Salt and pepper

1. Bring the tomato juice to the boil, remove from the heat, add the jelly cubes and leave them to dissolve. Stir.
2. Add the lemon juice, a few shakes of Worcestershire Sauce and salt and pepper.
3. Allow to cool before adding all the remaining ingredients.
4. Pour into a greased mould or individual ramekins and chill for several hours.
5. Serve with brown bread and butter and extra prawns.

SERVES 8

'**Everything I eat has been proved by some doctor or another to be a deadly poison and everything I don't eat has been proved to be indispensable for life. But I go marching on.**'
George Bernard Shaw

General Sir Richard Dannatt
GCB CBE MC ADC Gen
CHIEF OF THE GENERAL STAFF 2006–2009

Pea and Ham Soup

1 onion, chopped
55g butter
3 sticks celery, chopped
1 large potato, peeled and chopped
1 leek, chopped
1 bunch mint
500g garden peas, petit pois or minted peas
1½ pints chicken stock
400g cooked ham or gammon, shredded

1. Melt the butter in a saucepan and add all the vegetables apart from the peas. Coat in the butter and add mint.
2. Cover and sweat vegetables for 10–15 minutes until softening but not colouring.
3. Add peas and stock and simmer, without a lid, for about 10 minutes, until potato is soft. Remove mint sprigs.
4. Whizz or liquidise until smooth then sieve.
5. Season with salt and pepper and add ham or gammon.

'An Army marches on its
stomach.'
Napoleon

Garden House School Gardening Club

The children in the Gardening Club enjoy coming to the beautiful grounds of the Royal Hospital and they have been allocated their own garden space, where they grow flowers and vegetables. They are guided and encouraged by our wonderful Head Gardener, Ron Wilmore, who nurtures their enthusiasm. What a rare opportunity in the middle of London!

Combined contributors:

Mrs Julia Adlard
Miss Dawn Poole
Miss Pandora Louis
Byron Soubra
Christopher Yu
Sam Lazarus
Valentin Deravin-Rummel
Alessandra Segat
Cosmo Hamwee
Jasper Peimings
George Warland
Maximillian Grayer

Illustrations by Max de Suarez d'Aulan – age 7

Garden House Vegetable Soup

250g (9 oz) potatoes
2 medium leeks
2 carrots
25g (1oz) butter
1 tablespoon of oil
1 pint of vegetable stock
Dried mixed herbs
300ml milk
Salt and ground black pepper

Wash and peel the potatoes and carrots and cut into chunks. Cut the dark top and roots off the leeks, wash thoroughly and slice. Place potatoes, leeks and carrots in large saucepan with the butter and oil. Heat gently and stir. Cook for 10 minutes and then carefully add the stock. Stir in the milk, herbs, and a little salt and pepper. Let the soup cook gently for 15 minutes more, then eat!

General the Lord Guthrie GCB LVO OBE DL
CHIEF OF THE DEFENCE STAFF 1997–2001, GOLD STICK-IN-WAITING

Chilled Consommé and Avocado

My contribution to this cookbook is a simple recipe and one which I would be capable of producing myself. I particularly recommend this during hot, summer weather.

1 tin Campbell's beef consommé (well chilled in the fridge)
1 ripe avocado
Sour cream
Paprika to garnish

1. Take the Campbell's beef consommé from the fridge and place the contents in small soup bowls.
2. Chop the ripe avocado into small pieces and place on top of the consommé.
3. Place a teaspoon of sour cream on top of the avocado and a sprinkling of paprika.
4. Serve this as soon as possible from the fridge.

'Food for thought is no
substitute for the real thing.'
Walt Kelly

Dame Kiri Te Kanawa ONZ DBE AC
OPERA SINGER

Stolen Fish Chowder
(New Zealand Fish Chowder)

1 onion
2 fresh chillies (mild or hot to taste)
30g butter
2 tbsp plain flour
1 tbsp mild curry powder
2 cups milk
1 cup coconut milk
3 cups (1 lb 6 oz) fresh seafood chopped i.e cod, mussels, salmon,
   scallops and lobster
1 tsp salt (to taste)

1. Fry onions and chillies in butter until cooked or glazed.
2. Add flour and curry powder. Keep stirring.
3. Add milk and coconut milk.
4. Add uncooked fish.
5. Do not let the mixture boil – the fish will cook in the sauce very quickly.

Tip:
Make sure the fish is raw and not previously frozen or steamed.
The sauce (mixture without the fish) can be made the day before.

SERVES 2–3

'Cookery is an art and by no means one to be taken lightly.'
Luciano Pavarotti

Nigella Lawson
CHEF

Watermelon, Feta and Black Olive Salad

1 small red onion
2–4 limes, depending on juiciness
1.5kg sweet, ripe watermelon
250g feta cheese
Bunch of fresh flat-leaf parsley
Bunch of fresh mint, chopped
3–4 tbsp extra virgin olive oil
100g pitted black olives
Black pepper

1. Peel and halve the red onion and cut into very fine half-moons and put in a small bowl to steep with the lime juice, to bring out the transparent pinkness in the onions and diminish their rasp. Two limes' worth should do it, but you can find the fruits disappointingly dried up and barren when you cut them in half, in which case add more.
2. Remove the rind and pips from the watermelon and cut into approximately 4 cm triangular chunks, if that makes sense (maths is not my strong point). Cut the feta into similar sized pieces and put them both into a large, wide shallow bowl. Tear off sprigs of parsley so that it is used like a salad leaf, rather than a garnish and add to the bowl along with the chopped mint.
3. Tip the now glowingly puce onions, along with their pink juices over the salad in the bowl, add the oil and olives, then using your hands toss the salad very gently so that the feta and melon don't lose their shape. Add a good grinding of black pepper and taste to see whether the dressing needs more lime. Hava Negila! The taste of Tel Aviv sunshine!

SERVES 8

© Nigella Lawson

'**When one has tasted
watermelon he knows what
the angels eat**'
Mark Twain

Tom Parker Bowles
FOOD COLUMNIST

Chicken and Sweetcorn soup

1.2 litres dark chicken stock
1 chicken, meat stripped from bones and shredded
2 corn on the cobs, kernels stripped from cob
2 spring onions, sliced
½ lemon, juice only
Tabasco sauce
Salt and pepper

1. Bring the stock to the boil in a large saucepan and simmer for 15 minutes, to reduce a little.
2. Add the corn kernels to the stock and cook for 2 minutes.
3. Stir in the shredded chicken and simmer for a further 5 minutes.
4. Add the spring onions and a dash of lemon juice. Season with a dash of Tabasco and salt and pepper to taste.

SERVES 4

'Good manners: The noise you don't make when you're eating soup'
Bennett Cerf, humourist

Gordon Ramsay

CHEF AND RESTAURATEUR

London Particular

Named after the thick fog (called "pea-soupers") that used to shroud the London skyline before we became environmentally conscious, this soup has reliably provided nourishing comfort during cold, wintry evenings. It was traditionally made with the stock from boiled ham and any leftover meat. However, you can make it with a fresh piece of smoked ham, which will lend its flavour to the broth and eliminate the need for ham stock.

250g dried split green peas
2 tbsp olive oil
1 medium onion, peeled and chopped
1 stick celery, trimmed and chopped
Few sprigs of thyme
1 bay leaf
250g smoked ham
About 1 litre water
Sea salt and freshly ground black pepper

1. Cover the dried split peas in cold water and leave to soak overnight.
2. The next day, heat the olive oil in a heavy-based pot over medium heat. Stir in the onions, celery and herbs and cook for 5–6 minutes until the onions are soft and the celery looks translucent.
3. Rinse and drain the peas thoroughly. Add to the pot and stir well. Nestle the ham among the peas and vegetables, then pour in enough water to cover. Bring the liquid to the boil then reduce the heat to a simmer. Skim off any froth or scum that rises to the surface of the liquid. Slowly cook the soup for about 2–2½ hours until the peas are soft.
4. Remove the ham from the soup and cut into small cubes. Whizz the soup in a blender, in two batches, to a desired consistency. (I prefer mine to be a little chunky so I only process two thirds of the soup, then mix the purée with the remainder). Add a little water if the overall soup is too thick. If the opposite is true, return it to the pan and simmer for a little longer until reduced and thickened.
5. Taste and adjust the seasoning with salt and pepper.
6. Return the ham pieces to the soup, reheat and serve hot.

SERVES 4

General Sir David Richards
KCB CBE DSO ADC Gen
CHIEF OF THE GENERAL STAFF 2009

Narial (Coconut), Tomato and Crab Shorba (Soup)

This delicious recipe came from the kitchens of the Maharana of Udaipur.

500g tomatoes, chopped
20g garlic, finely chopped
100g onion, finely chopped
2 bay leaves
50g leeks, finely chopped
1 or 2 curry leaves
4 cloves
5 crushed black peppercorns
100g chopped coriander
100ml coconut milk
50g prepared crab meat
3 tablespoons oil
1 teaspoon cumin
Salt to taste
Water

1. Heat the oil then add cumin, garlic, onion, leeks, curry leaves, cloves and black pepper. Sauté for a few minutes then mix in the chopped tomatoes.
2. Sauté again for a few minutes then add 1 litre of water and add bay leaves and coriander.
3. Cook for half an hour then strain through a sieve. Add crab meat and coconut milk and heat through gently.
4. Serve garnished with chopped coriander.

Delia Smith CBE
COOKERY WRITER AND BROADCASTER

Roasted Tomato Soup with a Purée of Basil

At first you're going to think, 'Why bother to roast tomatoes just for a soup?', but I promise you that once you've tasted the difference you'll know it's worth it – and roasting really isn't any trouble, it just means time in the oven.

1½ lb (700g) ripe red tomatoes
1 fat clove garlic, chopped
1 small bunch fresh basil leaves
1 x 4 oz (110g) potato
15 fl oz (425ml) boiling water
1 heaped teaspoon tomato purée
1 teaspoon balsamic vinegar
Approx 3 tablespoons extra virgin olive oil
Salt and freshly milled black pepper

To Garnish: Olive Croûtons

You will also need a solid, shallow roasting-tray approx. 13 x 13 inches (33 x 33cm)

Pre-heat the oven to gas mark 5, 375°F (190°C).

First of all skin the tomatoes by pouring boiling water over them, then leave them for 1 minute exactly before draining them and slipping off the skins (protect your hands with a cloth if necessary).
Now slice each tomato in half, arrange the halves on the roasting-tray, cut side uppermost, and season with salt and pepper.
Sprinkle a few droplets of olive oil on to each one followed by the chopped garlic and finally top each one with a piece of basil leaf (dipping the basil in oil first to get a good coating).
Now pop the whole lot into the oven and roast the tomatoes for 50 minutes – 1 hour or until the edges are slightly blackened – what happens in this process is that the liquid in the tomatoes evaporates and concentrates their flavour, as do the toasted edges.

About 20 minutes before the end of the roasting time, peel and chop the potato, place it in a saucepan with some salt, 15 fl oz (425 ml) of boiling water and the tomato purée and simmer for 20 minutes.

When the tomatoes are ready, remove them from the oven and scrape them with all their juices and crusty bits into a food processor (a spatula is best for this), then add the contents of the potato saucepan and whizz everything to a not-too-uniform purée.

If you want to, you can now sieve out the seeds but I prefer to leave them in as I like the texture.

Just before serving the soup – which should be re-heated very gently – make the basil purée by stripping the leaves into a mortar, sprinkling with ¼ teaspoon of salt, then bashing the leaves down with the pestle. It takes a minute or two for the leaves to collapse down and become a purée, at which point add 2 tablespoons of olive oil and the balsamic vinegar and stir well.

(If you make this in advance, store it in a cup with clingfilm pressed on to the surface; it will keep its colour even overnight.) To serve the soup, pour it into warmed serving-bowls and drizzle the basil purée on to the surface, giving a marbled effect. Then finally sprinkle with Olive Croûtons and serve straight away.

Olive Croûtons (Ciabatta)

4 medium slices ciabatta bread, weighing approx. 2 oz (50g) each
1 dessertspoon olive paste (available from supermarkets)
1 tablespoon olive oil

Pre-heat the oven to gas mark 5, 375°F (190°C).

First of all cut the slices of bread into small cubes, then place them in a bowl together with the olive oil and olive paste and stir them around to get a good coating of both.

Then arrange the croûtons on a small baking-sheet and put them in the oven to bake for 8–10 minutes – but please do put on a timer for this as 10 minutes pass very quickly and croûtons have a nasty habit of turning into cinders!

Then leave to cool on the baking-sheet and serve with Chilled Fennel Gaspacho or Roasted Tomato Soup.

Extracted from *Delia's Summer Collection*, published by BBC Books
Copyright © Delia Smith 1993. For more Delia recipes visit deliaonline.com

The Duchess of Wellington MBE

♛

PARK CORNER HOUSE

FROM HER GRACE THE DUCHESS OF WELLINGTON MBE

Gazpacho

8 large tomatoes, skinned, deseeded and chopped
4 level tablespoons stale breadcrumbs
2 tablespoons olive oil
2 tablespoons white wine vinegar
4 cloves of garlic, crushed
Chilled water
Salt and pepper

1. In a glass bowl soak the breadcrumbs in the olive oil, vinegar and garlic for an hour.
2. Transfer breadcrumbs mix and tomatoes to food processor with 250 ml chilled water. Whizz until smooth.
3. Transfer to a glass jug and dilute to required consistency with more chilled water.
4. Add salt and pepper to taste and chill for at least an hour.

Serve in bowls with an ice cube and a leaf or two of flat parsley.

SERVES 4

Timothy West CBE
ACTOR

Proper Tomato Soup

2 tablespoons olive oil
4 crushed garlic cloves
1 medium onion, finely chopped
4 medium tomatoes, ripe and red
1 teaspoon oregano
3 mugs water

1. Heat the olive oil over medium heat.
2. Add the garlic and onion and cook till softened but not browned.
3. Add tomatoes, oregano and water, then simmer till well cooked.
4. Ladle into individual serving bowls and sprinkle with mint or basil, and grated cheese for those who want it.

SERVES 4–6

‘**Never eat more than you can lift.**’
Miss Piggy

Sir Frank Williams
F1 MOTOR RACING TEAM PROPRIETOR

Pea Cappuccino

1 small leek
30g butter
200g thinly sliced potatoes
500ml chicken stock
350g frozen peas (a few reserved for garnish)
100ml cream

1. Chop white part of leek and fry in butter until soft then add potatoes, the chicken stock and simmer until the potatoes are tender.
2. Add frozen peas, salt and pepper and simmer for two minutes. The peas should still be brightly coloured.
3. Purée, and then sieve the soup into a clean saucepan.
4. Add stock or water until the soup is liquid but not too thin.
5. Lightly whip the cream.
6. Put a few reserved peas into the bottom of heated soup dishes (preferably glass) pour in the soup then carefully spoon over the cream and grind some black pepper over the top.

'There is no love sincerer
than the love of food.'
George Bernard Shaw

Baroness Thatcher LG OM PC FRS
PRIME MINISTER 1979–1990

Number 10 'Cabinet Lunch'

This is a typical luncheon which we would serve at No.10 when the Cabinet was holding a special policy working session. I liked the meal to be robust and fortifying – just like our discussions!

Spinach Soup

450g (1lb) spinach leaves
900ml (1.5pts) vegetable stock
15ml (1 tbsp) lemon juice
Dash of Tabasco
Swirl of double cream
Salt and pepper

1. Place the spinach, stock and lemon juice in a large saucepan and season.
2. Bring to the boil then reduce the heat and simmer for 10 minutes.
3. Remove from the heat and allow to cool slightly.
4. Place liquid into a blender and blend until smooth.
5. Return the liquid to the pan to heat, add Tabasco to taste and a good swirl of double cream to enrich.

British Beef and Horseradish Casserole

1.1kg (2.5 lbs) good British stewing steak
450g (1 lb) onions
45ml (3 tbsp) oil
1 medium sized clove of garlic – crushed
225g (8 oz) button mushrooms
25g (1 oz) plain flour
5ml (1 tsp) ground ginger
5ml (1 tsp) curry powder
5ml (1 tsp) dark muscovado sugar
600ml (1pt) beef stock
30ml (2 tbsp) Worcestershire Sauce
30ml (2 tbsp) creamed horseradish
45ml (3 tbsp) chopped parsley
Salt and pepper

1. Heat the oil in a casserole and add a few pieces of meat to brown and then place on a warm plate. Repeat this process until all the meat has been sealed.
2. Slice the onions and place them in the casserole to cook for three minutes.
3. Reduce the heat. Add the garlic and the mushrooms and cook for an extra 3–4 minutes making sure that the onions and garlic do not burn.
4. Stir in the flour, spices and sugar and cook for a further 2 minutes.
5. Add Worcestershire Sauce, stock and seasoning and bring to boil. Cover.
6. Place the casserole on the middle shelf of the oven at 170C/325F/Gas mark 3 for 2 hours until the meat is tender.
7. Add the creamed horseradish and cook for further 10 minutes.
8. Shortly before serving stir in the chopped parsley.

Serve with mashed potato and carrots.

Chocolate Mousse

175g (7 oz) plain chocolate
30ml (2 tbsp) strong black coffee
100g (4 oz) unsalted butter
4 eggs separated
15ml (1 tbsp) brandy
75g (3 oz) icing sugar

1. Place most of the chocolate with the coffee into a heatproof bowl over a pan of hot water until all the chocolate has melted then add the brandy and stir for another 2 minutes.
2. Remove from the heat and add the butter gradually, continuing to stir constantly. Leave to cool slightly.
3. Add the icing sugar and the egg yolks and whip well.
4. Meanwhile beat the egg whites until they are stiff and fold them into the mixture. Leave in the fridge overnight to chill.
5. Shortly before serving shave the remaining chocolate over the top of the mousse.

Serve with raspberries.

SERVES 6

Main Courses

Slow Roast Shoulder of Lamb and
    Balsamic Onions
Pan Fried Chicken with Mushroom
    Sauce on a Bed of Tagliatelle
Chicken in Creamy Yoghurt
Tipsy Spaghetti
Gingered Pork Fillet
Gourmet Shepherd's Pie
Smoked Haddock Coulibiac
Papeta per Eenda – Eggs on Potatoes
Fish Pie
Take-away Pizza
The Best Rice Salad in the World
Roast Chicken
Chilli Vaquero
Woodman's Stew
Beans à la Clarkson
Lancaster Gate Mince
Haddock à la Crème
Curzon Crumble
Beef Stroganoff
Beef Stew
Butternut Squash Goulash
Chicken Tonnato
Kentish Pigeon Pie
Moussaka
Dodi's Brazilian Fish Stew
Scallops with Caramelised Granny
    Smiths and Black Pudding in a
    Champagne Sauce
Bachelor Scrambled Eggs and Tomatoes
Fruity Pork Fillets with Root Purée
Porc Etienne Dubois aka Porc à la
    Crème
Steeped Chicken
Ratatouille

Cheese on Toast
Runner Bean Chutney
Grilled Tuna Steak
Slow-cooked Game Casserole
Congolese Chilli Peanut Chicken
Chicken or Turkey Boobs
Chicken in the Pot
Pork Fillets with Apples, Onions, Cider
    and Cream
Bouillabaisse
Fish Pie
My Boys' Rice Dish
Hotpot
Fish Cakes
Honeymoon Spaghetti
Chicken and Mushroom Pie
Butter Poached Chicken Breast,
    Saffron Risotto, Chorizo
    Dumpling and Pumpkin Purée
Tabouleh Salad
Duck Breasts with
    Blackcurrant Sauce and
    Gratin Dauphinoise
Salad of Crispy Duck with
    Mango, Chilli and Ginger
Baked Penne with Dolcelatte
    Cheese and Radicchio
Spaghetti, Raw Tomato and
    Rocket
Green Bean and Tomato
    Tagliatelle
Oeufs à la Tripe
Loin of Venison with Green
    Pepper Sauce
Coq au Vin
Pasta with Broccoli and Chilli

Paella
Steak, Guinness and Mushroom Pie
Lamb Cutlets Reform
Fish Pasties with French Tarragon
Shepherd's Pie
Smart Tart
Aji de Gallina – Chicken with Hot
    Peppers
Lamb Tagine with Almonds
Lamb Cutlets Shrewsbury
Braised Oxtail and Celeriac Mash
Stopwatch Eggs with Toasted
    Soldiers
Tuna and Cannellini Beans

Henry VIII's Crunchy Pasta
Venison Steak Diane
Lamb Vindaloo
Roasted Woodcock with Quail Eggs on
    Potato Rosti
Slow-cooked Roast Pork Belly
Retro Chicken with Mushrooms and
    Bacon
Spaghetti with Fresh Lobster

Tom Aikens
CHEF AND RESTAURATEUR

Slow Roast Shoulder of Lamb with Balsamic Onions

1 shoulder of lamb weighing 2.5 kilos
1 bunch of thyme washed
8 whole medium sized onions, peeled
2 bulbs garlic, peeled
250ml balsamic vinegar
2g sea salt
150ml olive oil

Depending on when you are going to be eating this dish, either lunch or dinner, you want to put it into the oven a meal before, so for lunch time you want to put it into the oven at 8am and for the evening I would put it in at around 2pm. It will take about 6 hours to cook but it is one of those dishes that do not need any attention at all. You need a large casserole with a lid.

If you like you can marinate the lamb leg for a day in the olive oil with 6–8 sprigs of thyme and some extra thinly sliced garlic. Before you cook the lamb, leave it out of the fridge for a good hour, if not two, so the meat is at room temperature.

1. If you have marinated the leg remove the thyme and garlic, then season with the salt and some fresh black pepper. If not, rub in the olive oil and then season with salt and pepper.
2. Put a little olive oil in the bottom of the casserole, add the lamb and the onions and drizzle with olive oil. Put into the oven at 180C/350F/Gas mark 4 for 15–20 minutes until the lamb and onions have coloured.
3. Remove the casserole from the oven, add about 8 sprigs of thyme along with the seasoned and oiled garlic, then turn the oven down to 110C/225F/Gas mark ¼ and cook for 5 hours with a lid on.
4. Remove the lid, add the balsamic vinegar and continue to cook for a further hour. Then remove the garlic from the pan and place onto a low heat to reduce any excess liquid that is in the pan. Baste the lamb and onions in this whilst it is reducing. Be careful that they do not stick or burn.

SERVES 6

Photograph: Andrew Twort

HRH Princess Alexandra KG GCVO
Pan-Fried Chicken with Mushroom Sauce on a Bed of Tagliatelle

4 chicken breasts
6 medium-sized Portobello mushrooms
8 baby courgettes
400g fresh tagliatelle
500ml basil pesto (chopped basil, extra virgin olive oil, crushed
    pine nuts, finely chopped, Parmesan or pecorino cheese,
    crushed garlic, sea salt)
500ml whole fat crème fraiche
Lemon juice
Butter
Light olive oil

1. Prepare basil pesto to taste and set aside in bowl.
2. Top and tail the washed courgettes and chop 8–10 mm thick on the diagonal.
3. Heat a large frying pan, add a tablespoon of oil and fry 4 mushrooms, cut into wedges. Add more oil if necessary then reduce heat to low until the juices run. Add a knob of butter, a squeeze of lemon juice and keep warm.
4. Wipe the pan with kitchen roll and heat, adding a teaspoon of oil. Cut the stalks off the remaining mushrooms, chop finely and sweat gently without adding more oil or butter. Stir in crème fraiche, return to the heat for 2 minutes, cover and keep warm.
5. Wash, trim and dry the chicken breasts, brush with oil then brown and seal in a hot frying pan. Put the chicken in a hot oven 180C/350F/Gas mark 4 for 8–12 minutes until cooked.
6. Take cooked chicken out and rest in a warm place for 6–8 minutes. Slice each breast into 4 but keep in shape and keep warm.
7. Boil a large pan of salted water, add a tablespoon of oil and the tagliatelle and cook for 2–4 minutes, to taste. Drain, toss in basil pesto and keep warm.
8. Quick-fry the courgettes in oil to golden colour, drain on kitchen paper and keep warm.
9. In a large, flat, oval dish cover the base with the tagliatelle and put a few mushroom wedges around the edge. Arrange the sliced chicken breasts along the centre, drizzle the mushroom sauce over

them and garnish with the fried courgettes.

Serve with fine green beans, spring carrots and freshly grated Parmesan cheese.

SERVES 4

Anjum Anand
CHEF AND FOOD WRITER

Chicken in Creamy Yoghurt

This recipe has been in my family for as long as I can remember and it has always been a firm favourite of mine. It is easy to cook and can be made with the minimum of spices and even less effort. As a bonus for the health-conscious amongst you, very little oil is used in the dish. Serve the chicken with some green vegetables, roti or naan.

1.3kg chicken, skinned and jointed into small pieces
2 tbsp vegetable oil
1 small onion, peeled and chopped
1–2 green chillies, slit (optional)
1 large or 2 small black cardamom pods
Handful of fresh coriander stalks and leaves, finely chopped

Marinade:
15g garlic (approximately 7 large cloves), peeled
20g fresh ginger, peeled
400ml plain yoghurt
4 tsp coriander powder
½–1 tsp red chilli powder
1 rounded tsp garam masala
2 tsp salt, or to taste
½ tsp cumin powder

1. Purée the garlic and ginger with some of the yoghurt to make a smooth paste, and then stir in the remaining marinade ingredients. Tip into a non-metallic bowl, add the chicken and leave to marinate in the fridge for as long as possible (I leave mine overnight). Bring back to room temperature before cooking.
2. Pour the chicken and the marinade into a large saucepan and place over a high heat.
3. Meanwhile, heat the oil in a small pan and fry the onions and chillies, if using, for about 6 minutes or until soft. Once done, add to the chicken along with the cardamom pods and continue cooking over a high heat for about 15–20 minutes until the watery curry becomes creamy and covers only one-third of the chicken.
4. Cover the pan and cook the chicken over a very low heat for a further 10–15 minutes until it is tender and the gravy is rich and creamy. Stir occasionally, making sure there is enough water in the

pan and adding a splash more if necessary. Stir in the coriander, check the seasoning and serve.

SERVES 6–8

Indian Food Made Easy by Anjum Anand (Quadrille Publishing 2007) Copyright © Anjum Anand 2007

Colonel Laura Bale RRC
MATRON ROYAL HOSPITAL CHELSEA

Tipsy Spaghetti

This recipe is perfect for when you come home from a very good drinks party or the cinema and find there is nothing for supper.

Spaghetti
A few anchovies
Fresh parsley
Pine nuts
1 lemon
Truffle flavoured olive oil
Salt and black pepper

1. Cook the spaghetti to your liking and while it is bubbling away dry fry a handful of pine nuts, watching carefully that they do not burn.
2. Finely chop the anchovies and a handful of fresh parsley.
3. Drain the spaghetti and add the anchovies, parsley, pine nuts and the grated zest of the lemon.
4. Drizzle over a good glug of truffle flavoured oil, mix well, season and serve.

Julian Barrow
ARTIST

Gingered Pork Fillet

1 pork fillet
8 tablespoons dark soy sauce
2 inch piece of root ginger
4 oz water chestnuts
1 clove garlic, chopped

1. Cut the pork fillet into thin slices, put into a bowl and cover with the soy sauce.
2. Peel and chop the ginger and garlic and sprinkle over the meat.
3. Leave to marinate for 2–3 hours, turning once or twice.
4. Heat a little sunflower in a frying pan or wok, remove the meat from the marinade and stir fry briskly for 5 minutes or until cooked.
5. You can add the remaining marinade when the meat is cooked but make sure it is cooked through thoroughly.
6. Add water chestnuts and more ginger if desired then heat through.

Serve with colourful vegetables and egg noodles.

SERVES 4

'Dining is and always was a
great artistic opportunity.'
Frank Lloyd Wright

Martin Bell OBE
WAR CORRESPONDENT AND POLITICIAN

Gourmet Shepherd's Pie

½ lb potatoes
2 onions
1 tin chopped tomatoes
½ lb best minced beef
Chopped olives
Mixed herbs
Salt and pepper

1. Boil half a pound of potatoes until thoroughly cooked. Mash well. (Nothing spoils a shepherd's pie more than lumpy potatoes or too thin a covering of them.) Do not economise. Add a generous knob of butter and a little milk or cream.
2. Chop 2 onions finely and fry until brown in the minimum of cooking fat. Add a tin of chopped tomatoes, chopped olives to taste, mixed herbs, salt and pepper.
3. Coat half a pound of best ground beef in flour. Add it to the mix and stir well.
4. Transfer the enhanced ground beef to an oven-proof dish. It is then ready for a generous covering of mashed potatoes.
5. The final effect will be improved by a sprinkling of cheddar cheese and a quartered fresh tomato on top.
6. Cook for 90 minutes at a moderate heat 180C/350F/Gas mark 4. Serve with a side garnish of Suffolk Regiment Malabar Chutney, available from Butterworth and Son and at the annual march past of the Regiment's old soldiers at Gibraltar Barracks, Bury St Edmunds on Minden Day, the Sunday nearest August 1st.

'As a child my family's menu
consisted of two choices:
take it or leave it.'
Buddy Hackett

Mary Berry
CHEF AND COOKERY WRITER

Smoked Haddock Coulibiac

This is a good family supper dish, easy to serve with a green leaf salad. You can now buy puff pastry made from real butter – it is delicious but a little softer to handle.

450g (1lb) undyed smoked haddock fillet, skin on
50g (2 oz) butter
1 large onion, chopped
225g (8 oz) chestnut mushrooms, cut into quarters
2 teaspoons curry powder
75g (3 oz) long grain rice
2 eggs, hard boiled
2 good tablespoons chopped parsley
1 x 500g packet puff pastry
1 egg, beaten

Easy mango sauce:
1 x 200ml tub crème fraiche
4 generous tablespoons mango chutney
2 tablespoons fresh chopped parsley

Pre-heat oven 200C/180C Fan/400F/Gas mark 6

1. First cook the haddock in a pan and cover with cold water. Bring to the boil, cover and lift to one side to allow to cool (do not remove the lid). The haddock will finish cooking in the residual heat.
2. Melt the butter in a pan, add onion and cook over a medium heat for about 10 minutes until soft. Add the mushrooms and toss over a high heat for a few moments. Sprinkle in curry powder and cook for a minute more, stirring.
3. Remove the haddock from the pan once cooked and set aside. Add the rice to the fish liquid, if not quite covered add a little more water. Boil according to packet instructions, usually about 12 minutes, until cooked. Drain well.
4. Flake the fish into fairly large pieces, removing any bones along the way and discard the skin.
5. Mix the drained rice, fish, curried vegetables and parsley together and season with salt and pepper to taste. Set aside until cold.

6. Roll out the pastry into a 14" square, lift onto a baking sheet lined with non-stick paper. Spoon half the rice mixture down on long side of the pastry (leaving a 2 inch/4cm gap around the edge). Arrange the hard boiled eggs on top of the rice and top with the remaining rice mixture.

7. Brush the outer edges of pastry with beaten egg and lift the pastry over the rice and seal the edges together. Decorate the coulibiac with pastry leaves and brush with beaten egg.

8. Bake in pre-heated oven for about 30 minutes until the pastry is golden brown.

9. Mix the sauce ingredients together and serve with hot slice of coulibiac.

SERVES 6

To prepare ahead:
Make up to 24 hours ahead, cover with cling film and keep in the fridge. Brush with beaten egg before cooking. To freeze, wrap raw coulibiac in cling film then foil and freeze for up to 2 months. Thaw before cooking.

Aga cooking:
Bake on the floor of the roasting oven for about 25-30 minutes.

Stressfree Kitchen by Mary Berry (Headline 2008) Copyright © Mary Berry

'Guests, like fish, begin to smell after three days.'
Benjamin Franklin

Baron Bilimoria CBE DL
COMMISSIONER OF THE ROYAL HOSPITAL AND FOUNDER COBRA BEER

Eggs on Potatoes – Papeta per Eenda

This simple Parsi dish is a family favourite.

½ kg potatoes (4 large)
1 large onion, finely sliced
4 eggs
3 tablespoons cooking oil
¼ teaspoon turmeric powder
Pinch of red chilli powder
Salt to taste

1. Peel potatoes and cut into thin slices.
2. Heat oil in a frying pan and fry onions until golden brown.
3. Add turmeric, chilli powder and salt and stir well.
4. Add potatoes and blend well.
5. Add a little water, stir, cover pan and cook for a few minutes. Stir from time to time to prevent mixture from sticking to the bottom of the pan. Sprinkle in a little extra water, as required.
6. Cover pan and cook on low heat until potatoes are done.
7. Spread the mixture evenly in the pan, crack eggs and drop whole eggs on top, cover pan and cook on low flame until eggs are set/firm. Serve hot.

You can cook the mixture in a shallow baking dish and bake in a moderate oven until the eggs are set. If preferred, the eggs may be well beaten and spread evenly on the potato mixture and allowed to set. The same method can be used to make eggs on chopped okras (ladies' fingers).

SERVES 4

'After a good dinner one can forgive anybody, even one's own relatives.'
Oscar Wilde

Rt. Hon. Tony Blair

PRIME MINISTER 1997–2007

Fish Pie

1 onion
600ml milk
300ml double cream
450g unskinned cod fillet
225g undyed smoked cod fillet
4 tbsp chopped flat-leaf parsley
Pinch grated nutmeg
4 eggs
100g butter
45g plain flour
1.25kg potatoes (King Edwards/Maris Piper)
1 egg yolk
Salt and pepper

1. Put the onion slices in a pan with 450ml of the milk, the cream, cod and smoked cod. Bring to the boil and simmer for 8 minutes. Strain the fish and put the liquid in a jug. When the fish is cool enough to handle, break it into large flakes, discarding the skin and bones and put in the base of a shallow ovenproof dish.
2. Hard-boil the eggs for 8 minutes, drain and leave to cool. Peel, cut into slices and arrange on top of the fish.
3. Melt 50g of the butter in a pan, add the flour and cook for 1 minute. Take the pan off the heat and gradually stir in the reserved cooking liquid. Return it to the heat and bring slowly to the boil, stirring all the time. Simmer for 10 minutes. Stir in the parsley and season. Pour the sauce over the fish and leave to cool. Chill in the fridge for 1 hour.
4. Boil the potatoes for 15–20 minutes. Drain, mash and add the rest of the butter, the egg yolk and season. Beat in the remaining milk to form a soft, spreadable mash.
5. Preheat the oven to 200C/400F/Gas mark 6. Spoon the potato over the filling and bake for 35–40 minutes.

James Blunt
SINGER SONGWRITER

From:	James Blunt
Sent:	30 April 2009 10:24
To:	Angela Currie
Subject:	James Blunt's recipe

Dear Angela,

I don't cook and I live a rather odd life on the road. This may not be what you want, but it may be an amusement placed somewhere discreetly and surrounded by wonderful recipes.

Pizza Supper

Ingredients:

A telephone (either mobile or landline – whichever you prefer)

Dial Tops Pizza

Order a delicious pepperoni, onion and sweetcorn pizza

Strum gently for 30 minutes

Wait for the bell to ring

Receive the piping hot pizza and eat immediately

Accompany with 1 can of Coke

Good luck in your labour of love,

Best wishes

James

Baroness Boothroyd OM PC
SPEAKER OF THE HOUSE OF COMMONS 1992–2000

The Right Honourable Baroness Boothroyd O.M., P.C.

House of Lords
London SW1A 0PW

The Best Rice Salad in the World

2 large green peppers
2 large red peppers
4 large tomatoes
8 oz cooked French beans
4 oz black olives, stoned
2 oz chopped walnuts
1 clove garlic, crushed
4 oz black or green grapes, stoned
4 oz sultanas soaked in boiling water for 30 minutes and drained
Juice of two large lemons
1 teaspoon chopped fresh thyme
1 teaspoon chopped fresh rosemary
Half a pint of double cream
4 oz long grain or brown rice cooked and allowed to become cold
Salt and pepper to taste

1. Slice tomatoes thinly without skinning and mix well with crushed garlic.
2. Slice peppers in quarter inch strips.
3. With the exception of lemon juice and cream mix all ingredients together.
4. Chill for an hour or two.
5. When ready to serve pour over lemon juice, then cream. I often leave out the cream as it is so fattening. But it is delicious!

This recipe can be adjusted so as not to waste left-over rice. After all we all tend to be rather heavy handed when cooking rice!

SERVES 6

Peter Bowles
ACTOR

Roast Chicken

This is one of my favourite dishes; you cannot beat a simple roast chicken for guaranteed pleasure.

3 lb fresh chicken
Oil and butter
1 lb potatoes
1 stock cube
1 tbsp plain flour
Salt and pepper

1. Peel the potatoes and par-boil for about 5 minutes. Drain and put aside.
2. Put chicken in roasting pan, rub with oil and butter then add salt and pepper.
3. Cook chicken at 190C/375F/Gas mark 5 for about an hour. The chicken doesn't need fancy stuffing or herbs but just a lovely crispy skin when cooked, and the butter guarantees this.
4. 40 minutes before the chicken is finally cooked, cut the potatoes into small pieces and roll in oil and butter. Place in a shallow roasting tin and put in the oven.
5. Dissolve the stock cube in boiling water and take the cooked chicken out of the roasting pan. Leave to rest.
6. Stir the flour into the residue juices left in the roasting pan and stir until well mixed and brown. Add stock, stirring continuously whilst bringing to the boil and you have your gravy!
7. Serve with cooked vegetables of your choice.

SERVES 4

'A man may be a pessimistic determinist before lunch and an optimistic believer in the will's freedom after it.'
Aldous Huxley

Fred Brunger and Nick Clark
CHELSEA PENSIONERS

Chilli Vaquero

In 2008 Chelsea Pensioners Fred Brunger and Nick Clark braved a long journey to Guyana where Nick's old army mate Edwin Joseph now lives. In fact Fred had served there in the 1950s with the REME – when it was known as British Guiana. They laid a wreath on Remembrance Sunday at the national memorial in honour of Commonwealth soldiers who died in combat.

The local Amerindian cowboys are known as *vaqueros* and this is a favourite dish which Fred and Nick enjoyed during their visit.

1kg minced beef
2 large onions
2 cloves garlic
2 large hot chilli peppers, seeded and chopped
 or 1 teaspoon chilli powder
2 tablespoons oil
2 tablespoons sultanas or raisins
4 large tomatoes
3 large sweet peppers, 2 green and 1 red
4 cloves
1 teaspoon salt and freshly ground black pepper
1 tablespoon oregano or basil, chopped
3 tablespoons chopped stuffed green olives

1. Peel and slice the onions and peel and crush the garlic. Brown gently in the oil.
2. Add the minced beef and stir fry till lightly browned.
3. Prepare the chilli and add to the cooking meat mixture.
4. Chop the tomatoes roughly and deseed and slice the sweet peppers.
5. Add tomatoes, sultanas, cloves, herbs and seasonings to meat in pan.
6. Cook for 15 minutes stirring frequently.
7. Stir in the peppers and chopped olives and cook for 5 minutes more.
8. Garnish with stuffed olives and serve with salad, peas and rice or mashed sweetcorn with crushed boiled and sweet potatoes.

SERVES 4

Viscount Chelsea
CHAIRMAN OF THE FRIENDS OF THE ROYAL HOSPITAL CHELSEA

Woodsman's Stew

A large part of my adult life has been spent serving as an officer in the regular and then Territorial Army. Consequently, I am extremely interested in military history, not so much in the facts (the dates and places), but more on the life and experiences of officers and soldiers through the ages.

This recipe started formulating in my mind when I was reading the personal accounts of Major Robert Rogers and Private William Kirkwood both serving in the British Army during the French-Indian War of 1756-63 in New England, North America. Frontiersmen, woodsmen and soldiers alike had to be resilient, intuitive and above all adaptable to survive the harsh landscape and climate. Reading deeper into their journals I took particular interest in the food that they carried on long patrols into the dense forests. This mainly consisted of Bologna sausage, dried beans, dried peas, onions, salt, rice, potatoes and Indian corn flour. In addition, they supplemented these rations by hunting game during such patrols (tactical situation permitting). In one of the journals Kirkwood described mixing in the camp kettle some of the contents of their food rations to produce a very hearty stew after a long day's march. I began wondering what this food was really like; could it be better than our modern day rations, or the dehydrated camping food you buy in shops?

Intrigued, I decided to experiment whilst in the woods up in Scotland with my two young sons and we set about recreating a version of what Kirkwood described in his journals. The product of our endeavours was a resounding success. This hearty stew was delicious, so much so that I trialled it on two of my close military friends. They agreed that it was outstandingly tasty and as a result they have rethought what food they carry in the field, especially as if kept dry, these rations (as carried by the men of the mid-18th century) last a very long time in your pack.

So here's how to prepare a perfect Woodsman's Stew:

'One cannot think well, love
well, sleep well, if one has
not dined well.'
Virginia Woolf

Equipment:
1x small billy-can (pot holding approx. 2½ pints)
1x wooden spoon

Ingredients:
1x salami-type sausage (Karbanosi is good)
2–3 medium sized potatoes
2 medium sized onions
½ a cup full of dried beans (any type)
½ a cup full of dried peas
1x vegetable stock cube

Preparation:
2 or 3 hours prior to your evening meal in the woods, steep the beans and the peas in the billy-can in a pint of water and put to one side. Get a medium sized camp fire well and truly established with a good heat base. Finely chop/slice the sausage, potatoes and onion into the billy-can and add the beans and peas. Top up the billy can with water so that the level just covers the food. Break and mix in the vegetable stock cube. Place the billy-can over the fire on your pot-hang. Bring to boil and then simmer for between 15 and 20 minutes, stirring occasionally, and when the potatoes are soft the woodsman's stew is ready.

To gain the full effect of Woodsman's Stew it has to be prepared on an open fire and eaten outside in the woods. It has certainly revolutionised the way I think about camping food and there are many variations that can be made to the theme. After a long, hard day out in the hills my sons and I never tire of the treat of a Woodsman's Stew to look forward to.

Jeremy Clarkson
MOTORING BROADCASTER AND JOURNALIST

Beans à *la* Clarkson

My great, great, great grandfather was John Kilner (1792-1852) and he invented Kilner Jars, used to preserve foods in the days before we all had deep freezers. My father-in-law, Robert Henry Cain, received a Victoria Cross for actions during Operation Market Garden at Arnhem in World War II.

1 tin of Heinz Baked Beans (only Heinz – no imitations allowed)
Lashing of butter
6 Drops of Tabasco
Good white bread

1. Find a can opener, open tin of beans, put in a saucepan with two large knobs of butter and the Tabasco.
2. Heat the beans slowly over a low heat for a long time until the mixture becomes slightly mushy, the beans must still just resemble the shape of a bean but the mixture must be mushy.
3. Place two slices of bread in the toaster and toast lightly. Butter the toast liberally, making sure that the butter reaches every corner.
4. Place the beans all over the toast and serve immediately.

'When a man entered a soldier's life, he should have parted with half his stomach.'
Sergeant J S Cooper 7th Royal Fusiliers, Wellington's Army

Wendy Cope
POET

Lancaster Gate Mince

I learned this recipe 40 years ago from a flatmate, who had learned it from a friend, who was under the impression that it is Arabian. I don't know about that but it is very nice and I still cook it sometimes. In Lancaster Gate we used to peel fresh tomatoes but I can't be bothered with that nowadays. I often put in a red pepper, as well as the green one. This is the amount I do for two people but we don't have any carbohydrates with it, just a green salad or some green beans. If you're eating it with potatoes, rice or couscous, you won't need as much meat.

1 tablespoon cooking oil
1 onion, chopped
1 large green pepper, deseeded and chopped
400g minced beef
400g tin chopped tomatoes
1 heaped teaspoon dried mixed herbs
Salt and pepper

1. Heat the oil and fry the onion for a few minutes.
2. Add the pepper and fry for another minute or two.
3. Add the mince, breaking it up with a spoon and stirring it about until it is all brown.
4. Add the tomatoes, herbs and seasonings, stir, and cook gently for another 15–20 minutes.

'**Any healthy man can go without food for two days but not without poetry.**'
Charles Baudelaire

HRH The Duchess of Cornwall

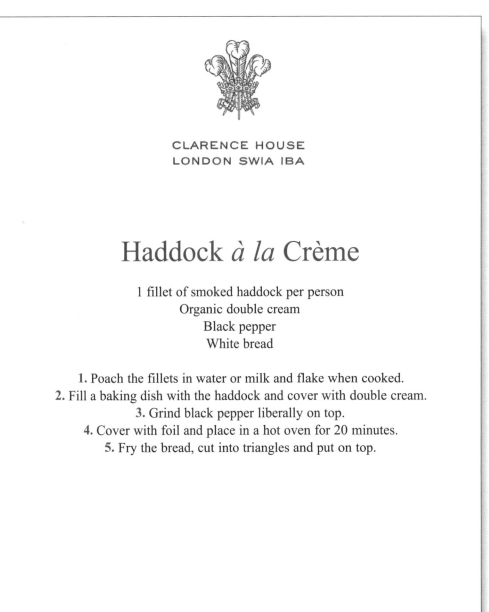

CLARENCE HOUSE
LONDON SW1A 1BA

Haddock *à la* Crème

1 fillet of smoked haddock per person
Organic double cream
Black pepper
White bread

1. Poach the fillets in water or milk and flake when cooked.
2. Fill a baking dish with the haddock and cover with double cream.
3. Grind black pepper liberally on top.
4. Cover with foil and place in a hot oven for 20 minutes.
5. Fry the bread, cut into triangles and put on top.

Lady Mary Gaye Curzon
Curzon Crumble

This is a really delicious dish for a wintry Sunday lunch but I can't do quantities. It is fairly straightforward and I think anyone could happily give it a try.

2 oven-ready pheasants
1 onion, sliced
Tub of mushrooms
Red wine
Packet of bacon
3–4 slices of bread
2 garlic cloves, chopped
Butter and plain flour
Salt and pepper

1. Pop some butter and onion inside the pheasants, cover the breasts with a couple of slices of bacon and roast for about 45 minutes at 200C/400F/Gas mark 6 until cooked.
2. Cut the meat off the pheasants, putting bite-sized pieces in the bottom of an ovenproof dish.
3. Fry the sliced mushrooms and garlic then spread them over the pheasant meat.
4. Make a roux with butter and plain flour and stir in all the juices from the roasting pan and plenty of red wine. Stir until thickened and smooth.
5. Pour the red wine sauce over the pheasant and mushrooms.
6. Fry chopped bacon with breadcrumbs in butter and spread over the top of the dish.
7. Bake the crumble at 190C/375F/Gas mark 5 for 20 minutes or until it is golden brown on the top.

'A good cook is like a
sorceress who dispenses
happiness.'
Elsa Schiaparelli

General Sir Richard Dannatt
GCB CBE MC ADC Gen
CHIEF OF THE GENERAL STAFF 2006 – 2009

Beef Stroganoff

'I can't cook to save my life but this is what I'd cook if I could'.

450g/1 lb beef fillet
55g/2 oz butter
2 shallots, finely sliced
1 garlic clove, crushed
225g/7 ½ oz field mushrooms, sliced
150g/5 oz dried porcini, soaked in 100ml chicken stock
100ml/3 fl oz white wine
150ml/5 fl oz chicken stock
1 tbsp oil
3 tbsp brandy
2 tbsp double cream
2 tbsp full fat crème fraiche

1. Cut the beef fillet into finger thick strips about 2 inches long.
2. Heat a large frying pan or wok. Melt half the butter, add shallots and cook over a low heat until soft and transparent.
3. Strain dried mushrooms, reserving liquor, and add them, together with the fresh mushrooms to the shallots and cook 1–2 minutes.
4. Add wine, stock and mushroom liquor. Continue to cook for at least 5 minutes until liquids have reduced to 3 tablespoons.
5. Remove from pan to a bowl.
6. Heat the oil and remaining butter in the frying pan. Dry meat, season and add to hot pan and fry off quickly to brown the edges but not to cook through. Remove to bowl.
7. Pour brandy into pan and ignite. Wait for flames to subside (have lid nearby in case flames get out of control!)
8. Add mushroom and stock mix, cream and crème fraiche and reduce on high heat until syrupy.
9. Return meat to the pan to reheat.
10. Serve on a platter with extra crème fraiche.

Clarissa Dickson Wright

CHEF

Beef Stew

900g stewing steak
Flour for coating, seasoned with salt, pepper, mustard powder
    and cayenne pepper,
50g beef dripping or cooking oil
100g bacon
4 onions, roughly chopped
300ml draught cider
25g black treacle
100g celery, chopped
4 tinned anchovy fillets
Sprig of thyme
75g pickled walnuts, roughly chopped
600ml beef stock

For the dumplings:
225g plain flour
½ teaspoon baking powder
Salt and pepper
100g suet

1. Cut the meat into 2.5 cm pieces and coat with the seasoned
flour by shaking the meat and flour together in a plastic bag.
2. Heat the dripping in a pan and add the coated meat cubes.
Seal the meat and cook until brown, then remove to a stew pan.
3. Chop the bacon, cook it with the onions in the pan until the
onions are soft. Remove to the stew pan. Add all the other
ingredients, cover and cook for 2 hours, stirring occasionally
or cook in the oven at 160C/325F/Gas mark 3.
4. For the dumplings, sift the flour with the baking powder, a pinch
of salt and a grind of pepper. Mix in the suet and enough cold
water to make a stiff dough. Make the dumpling mixture into balls
and add to the stew 30 minutes before the end of cooking.

SERVES 4

Clarissa's Comfort Food by Clarissa Dickson Wright (Kyle Cathie 2008) © Clarissa Dickson Wright

Sir James Dyson

INVENTOR AND ENTREPRENEUR

Butternut Squash Goulash

This is a vegetarian dish that we both love. It is quite rustic but served in a deep modern dish with crusty bread can look wonderful with its golden colour.

1 tablespoon of olive or sunflower oil
1 onion roughly chopped
1 red pepper, deseeded and cut into chunks
1 clove of garlic, crushed or chopped
2 teaspoons paprika
1 teaspoon caraway seeds
375g/12 oz butternut squash or pumpkin, thickly sliced
1 large carrot, thickly sliced
75g/3 oz red or green lentils
450ml/ ¾ pint vegetable stock
4 teaspoons tomato purée
1 teaspoon sugar
Salt and pepper
Crusty bread to serve

To garnish:
4 tablespoons half-fat crème fraiche or natural yoghurt
Paprika
Caraway seeds

1. Heat the oil in a large, flameproof casserole, add the onion and fry for 5 minutes until lightly browned.
2. Add the red pepper, garlic, paprika and caraway seeds and cook, stirring for 1 minute.
3. Add the pumpkin, carrot, lentils, stock, tomato purée, sugar, salt and pepper.
4. Bring to the boil, cover and cook in a preheated oven 180C/350F/Gas mark 4 for one hour.
5. To serve, spoon the goulash into bowls then top with 2 tablespoonfuls of crème fraiche or yoghurt and a sprinkling of paprika and caraway seeds.
Serve with chunks of crusty bread.

Julian Fellowes
ACTOR AND SCREENWRITER

Chicken Tonnato

Cooked chicken breast meat
Large tin of tuna
Mayonnaise
Cream
Capers
Lemon juice
Salt and pepper

1. This is a slight cheat, but it is really for people who think Vitella Tonnato is delicious but they are uncomfortable eating veal. It also has the supreme merit of being prepared in about two seconds flat, with supplies hastily purchased from your local grocer.

2. Take as many thin slices of cooked, white chicken as you need to feed whoever's coming. To be honest, this doesn't really work with the dark meat so it ought to be breast. Again, you can buy it cooked, but don't slice it too soon or it dries out.

3. Put the contents of a large tin of tuna into your whizzer (I think the tuna in sunflower oil tastes nicer than the brine, but this is only an opinion). Add equal quantities of mayonnaise and cream. I think single cream works best as otherwise it all gets a bit clammy, but you must be the judge of that. Then turn it on. After it's been made into a smooth, creamy sauce, add a pudding spoon of lemon juice and salt and pepper to taste.

4. Arrange the slices of chicken in a serving dish, pour the sauce evenly over the whole thing and then add some chopped capers (or just capers) to the top. You want a reasonable amount of these, but don't smother it.

And Bob's your uncle!

It is very tasty with hot, new potatoes in butter and a green salad in a light dressing. In truth, for a summer lunch party, I don't think it's beatable. But then I would say that, wouldn't I?

Frederick Forsyth
AUTHOR

Kentish Pigeon Pie

The wild woodpigeon is looked down upon by British townies, but wrongly. The French, who know a bit about cuisine, usually have 'pigeon roti' or 'pigeonneau' on the best menus.

The meat starts out dry and hard, because the wild pigeon is supremely fit. Thus it has to be tenderised and moisturised.

It is also 100% fat-free, cholesterol-free, healthy and very nutritious. Plus, tasty. And very economical. This recipe is for one bird/one portion. Multiply in proportion.

Take one bird from the poulterer, unplucked. Do not pluck the whole bird. A waste of time. The meat is in the two breasts only.

Strip the breasts of feathers, cut away with a very sharp knife. Peel off surplus skin. This leaves two steaklets Pound flat with rolling pin, dunk in marinade of cheap port over-night.

Prepare earthenware casserole thus: tablespoon olive oil, diced Spanish onion. Wrap breasts inside streaky bacon rashers (to impregnate with moisture) and pin closed with toothpick.

Complete with diced turnip/parsnip/swede cubes and carrot chunks. Top up with port marinade and equal quantity of water. Dust with two teaspoons Bisto beef.

Cover and simmer twelve hours in lower Aga. Re-cover with shortcrust/puff pastry, hot grill for ten minutes until crunchy and brown. Serve with minted peas and new potatoes. And a decent claret on a winter's day.

Frederick Forsyth.

Paddy Fox BEM
CHELSEA PENSIONER

Moussaka

Paddy Fox conducts numerous tours around the Royal Hospital, amusing all the visitors with his banter and jokes; his favourite dish of all time is Moussaka.

3 large aubergines
2 medium onions
4 cloves garlic, crushed
1kg minced lamb
400g tinned tomatoes
100ml red wine
2 tbsp tomato purée
Olive oil
2 tbsp chopped oregano
75g butter
75g plain flour
600ml milk
50g Parmesan cheese, grated
2 medium eggs, beaten
Salt and pepper, pinch of grated nutmeg, cinnamon stick

1. Cook the onions and garlic in oil until browned, add the mince and fry over high heat, stirring, for about 5 minutes.
2. Add the red wine, tomato purée, tinned tomatoes, cinnamon and oregano and simmer gently for 30–40 minutes, stirring occasionally.
3. Slice the aubergines, brush with olive oil and fry in batches until browned. Lay half the slices in the bottom of a shallow ovenproof dish and season well.
4. Remove the cinnamon stick from the sauce and spoon half the mixture over the aubergines. Repeat with the remaining aubergines and sauce.
5. Melt the butter in a pan, add the flour and cook for 1 minute. Slowly beat in the milk until slightly thickened then simmer for 10 minutes. Stir in the cheese and nutmeg, season. Cool slightly then stir in the eggs and pour the topping over the lamb and bake for 30–40 minutes at 200C/400F/Gas mark 6 until golden brown and bubbling.

SERVES 6

Mel Giedroyc
Performer and Writer

Dodi's Brazilian Fish Stew

My sister-in-law Dodi always cooks for tons of people and this is a failsafe crowd-pleaser. Sorry these ingredients don't come with very specific measures – Dodi's not that kind of woman!

2 good-sized skinned fillets of white fish (I use cod or haddock)
1 good-sized skinned fillet of smoked fish (smoked haddock
    is perfect)
Cooked prawns (I buy a bag of frozen prawns and defrost them)
1 medium to large onion, chopped
Olive oil
2 cans chopped tomatoes or fresh tomatoes if you prefer
1 tin coconut milk
Lots of fresh coriander
Salt and lots of freshly ground black pepper

1. Heat the olive oil in a big stew pan and cook the chopped onion.
2. Add the fillets of white and smoked fish and break them down into good-sized chunks as they cook. Keep the fish moving so that it doesn't stick. It should cook until it's getting flaky, then add the chopped tomatoes.
3. Bring to a simmer and then add the coconut milk. You don't want to drown your stew with coconut and make it so pale that it tastes sickly. I usually find that two-thirds of a tin is enough for this amount of fish. The colour of your stew should become a rich, reddish pink, not a pastel, marshmallow pink.
4. Bring to a gentle boil, throw in the prawns and cook through.
5. Season with lots of freshly ground black pepper and fresh coriander. Dodi puts the stalks in too.
Serve with rice.

'To eat is a necessity, to eat
intelligently is an art.'
La Rochefoucauld

The Hairy Bikers
CHEFS

Scallops with Caramelised Granny Smiths and Black Pudding in a Champagne Sauce

15 king scallops (5 per portion), corals removed
Sea salt and ground black pepper
150ml Champagne
100ml cream
1 tbsp Dijon type mustard
75ml good fish stock
1 tbsp flat leaf parsley, chopped
50g butter + knob of butter
2 tsp olive oil
Black pudding, cut into rounds – the sausage shaped Stornaway
    type is best for us
3 Granny Smith apples
1 tbsp soft brown sugar

1. In a large frying pan melt 50g butter, add the shallots and soften, then deglaze with Champagne.
2. Reduce the Champagne by half then add the fish stock, cream and mustard. Reduce until you get the required consistency for the sauce.
3. Peel and core the apples, cutting into rings about ½ cm thick. Heat the oil and knob of butter in a frying pan and add the sugar, stirring until bubbling. Add the apple slices and cook on both sides until caramelised. Set aside.
4. On a hot griddle pan cook the rounds of black pudding. Set aside to keep warm.
5. Coat the scallops in oil and season lightly. Retaining the black pudding fatty juices in the hot griddle pan, heat to smoking hot and sear the scallops until they start to caramelise. Remove and set aside.
6. Stir the chopped parsley into the Champagne sauce and warm to the desired temperature. Check and adjust the seasoning then keep warm.
7. Place a round of black pudding on top of a Granny Smith ring. Top with a scallop and a smear of Champagne sauce.

SERVES 3

Rolf Harris CBE AM
ENTERTAINER AND ARTIST

Bachelor Scrambled Eggs and Tomatoes

2 eggs per person
Spring onion, finely chopped (optional)
Butter
2 tomatoes per person
Milk
Salt and pepper

1. Melt a splodge of butter in a frying pan and drop in the spring onion. Cook over slow heat for a short while. Then add a slosh of milk, but not too much or the eggs will be watery later. Remove from the heat and break the eggs into the pan. Add a dusting of salt to each egg and as much pepper as you enjoy.
2. Return to the low heat and graunch up the eggs with a wooden spoon and generally scramble them around. The heat must be low – nothing is worse than those little black horribly burnt bits in scrambled egg.
3. Meanwhile, cut your tomato in half and place under the grill. Put the flat side down first and grill until the skin shrivels up and starts to go black. Then turn over, add a dusting of salt and grill the flat side.
4. Your scrambled eggs should be just starting to solidify, so take it off the heat for a tick whilst you pop in your two beautifully grilled tomatoes. The skin on the smooth side just comes away but you will need to cut out the core of the tomato.
5. Return to the heat while you squelch up the tomato into bite sized pieces with the wooden spoon.
6. Don't dry it up too much.

DELICIOUS!

Ainsley Harriott
CHEF

Fruity Pork Fillets with Root Purée

For the mash:
8 oz parsnips, cubed
8 oz floury potatoes, cubed
3–4 tablespoons milk
1½ oz butter
Salt and freshly ground black pepper

For the pork:
8 oz tenderloin pork fillet, cut into 2 inch slices
1 tablespoon flour, seasoned with salt and pepper
2 oz butter
8 ready to eat prunes soaked for at least thirty minutes
    in dry white wine
1 tablespoon of cranberry or redcurrant jelly
5 fl oz of double cream
Juice of 2 lemons
Salt and pepper

1. Cook parsnips and potatoes in a large pan of boiling, salted water for 10–12 minutes until tender.
2. Dust the pork with the seasoned flour. Heat half the butter in a large frying pan and when foaming, cook the pork for 1–2 minutes on each side. Remove and set aside.
3. Strain the wine into a hot pan and bring to the boil. Stir in the redcurrant jelly and cook for a further two minutes, until melted.
4. Add the cream, prunes and pork, season to taste and gently simmer until the pork is cooked through.
5. Drain the root vegetables and mash well. Add the milk and remaining butter and whizz with an electric hand whisk until smooth and puréed. Season to taste.
6. Squeeze a little lemon juice into the pork pan and check the seasoning. Pile the mash on to serving plates and spoon over the pork mixture.

Serve with green beans.

SERVES 2

85

Professor Richard Holmes CBE TD JP

HISTORIAN

Porc Etienne Dubois aka Porc *à la* Crème

This dish was a useful standby when I was a bachelor in the mists of time. The recipe was given to me by my old friend Stephen Wood, hence its name.

1½ lb pork fillet or boned loin or spare rib of pork
2 tablespoons cooking oil
1 oz butter (I generally use a bit more)
2 medium size or large onions
1 level tablespoon paprika
1 level tablespoon flour
1 beef stock cube plus ½ pint water
At least 5 tablespoons sherry
A good tablespoon tomato purée
6 oz small mushrooms or larger ones cut into large chunks
1 level teaspoon cornflour
5 oz double cream
Croutons and parsley to garnish

First, drink the remnants of the bottle of sherry to get into the right frame of mind.

1. Cut the pork into 1½ inch pieces. Heat the oil in a robust iron pan by well-known French manufacturer, add butter and then fry pork pieces quickly till they begin to brown.
Remove pieces from pan, and drain.
2. Fry onion and paprika for 2 minutes, blend in the flour and cook for another minute. Remove from heat and blend in the stock. Add sherry and tomato purée, return to heat and simmer till thick – perhaps 5–6 minutes. Season with salt and pepper, add meat.
3. Cover pan and simmer till pork is tender, about 30–40 minutes.
4. At the end of cooking time add the mushrooms. Blend cornflower into a smooth paste with two tablespoons cold water and add to pan.
5. Bring up to boil, and then allow to cool a little before stirring in the cream. Do not overdo the stirring in. You just want to turn the colour from brownish to pinkish. Decorate with the croutons and the parsley. Good served with mashed potatoes or rice.

SERVES 4

Ken Hom OBE
CHEF

Steeped Chicken

This is a classic Cantonese chicken dish (also known as White Cut Chicken) which my mother often made. The technique used is called steeping, which applies to delicate foods, such as chicken. Here the gentlest possible heat is used so that the flesh of the chicken remains extremely moist and flavourful with a satiny almost velvet-like texture. It is not difficult to make. The chicken simmers in liquid for a few minutes, then the heat is turned off, the pot tightly covered, and the chicken left to steep to finish cooking.

1 x 1.5-1.75kg (3½–4 lb) free-range or cornfed chicken
6 slices fresh ginger
6 whole spring onions
1 tablespoon salt and freshly ground black pepper, to taste

Cantonese-Style Dipping Sauce:
The pure, simple flavours of White-Cut Chicken call for a suitably pungent counterpoint in the dipping sauce. Spring onions and ginger root, jolted to the full fragrance by a quick dousing of hot peanut oil, offer the perfect flavour combination.

4 tablespoons spring onions, white part only, finely chopped
2 teaspoons fresh ginger, finely chopped
2 teaspoons salt
2 tablespoons groundnut or peanut oil

1. Rub the chicken evenly with the salt. In a pot large enough to hold the chicken, put the chicken in, cover with water and bring to a boil. Add the spring onions and ginger. Cover tightly and reduce the heat and simmer for 20 minutes. Then turn off the heat and leave covered tightly for 1 hour.
2. To make the sauce, place all of the ingredients in a stainless bowl and mix well. Heat a wok until it is hot and add the oil. When the oil is very hot and smoking, pour it on the sauce ingredients and mix well. The sauce is now ready.
3. Remove the chicken to a chopping board. Strain and save the liquid which can be used as a base for making stock or use it to cook rice. Cut the chicken into bite-sized pieces and arrange it on a platter. Serve the sauce on the side.

SERVES 4

Katherine Jenkins

SINGER AND 'CHELSEA PENSIONERS' SWEETHEART'

Ratatouille

2 tablespoons olive oil
2 large onions sliced
1 medium aubergine, chopped into cubes
1 red pepper, chopped
1 green pepper, chopped
2 cloves garlic
2 medium courgettes, sliced
2 x 400g cans chopped tomatoes
1 tablespoon tomato purée
3 fl ozs port
1 tablespoon honey
1 oz brown sugar
1 tablespoon white vinegar
Salt and pepper

1. Heat the oil in a large saucepan and cook the onions gently for 5 minutes until softened.
2. Add the crushed garlic and tomato purée and cook for a further 2 minutes.
3. Add all the other ingredients and bring to the boil.
4. Cover and simmer for around 20 minutes until the vegetables are *al dente*.
5. Serve with rice or on its own with Parmesan cheese sprinkled on top.

Parmesan cheese has been around for much longer than we realise. Samuel Pepys buried, 'my Parmesan cheese, as well as my wine' in his garden in Fleet Street, to protect them from the Great Fire of London in 1666. Parmesan makes everything taste better (umami). Napoleon, with all the French cheeses on offer, still chose Parmesan and when desperately ill, Moliere refused broth but ate Parmesan so greedily that it spilt over his deathbed.

Boris Johnson
POLITICIAN AND MAYOR OF LONDON

Cheese on Toast

1. Grate large amount of cheese, preferably Cheddar
2. Lightly toast brown bread
3. Lavish toast with butter
4. Cover toast with grated cheese
5. Grill until it browns nicely

Good luck!

'Many is the long night I
dreamed of cheese –
toasted, mostly.'
Robert Louis Stevenson

Professor Ajay Kakkar BSc MBBS PhD FRCS

PROFESSOR OF SURGICAL SCIENCES AND THE LONDON SCHOOL OF MEDICINE

Runner Bean Chutney

This is a family recipe. My wife Nicky was given the recipe by her mother, who was given it, in turn, by her mother.

2 lbs (1kg) runner beans
4–5 onions
1½ tbsp each of mustard, cornflour and turmeric
1½ pints (850 ml) malt vinegar
2 lbs (1kg) granulated sugar

1. Slice the onions and beans and boil gently in salted water until tender.
2. Strain and chop up.
3. Return to the pan with 700ml (1¼ pints) vinegar and boil for 15 minutes.
4. Mix remaining ingredients together, add to the saucepan and boil for a further 15 minutes.
5. Pot up straight away.

Makes about 5 x 1 lb pots.

This chutney could be the ideal accompaniment to some of the other recipes in this book such as Ainsley Harriott's Fruity Pork Fillets with Root Purée (page 85), Anton Mosimann''s Fish Cakes (Page 105), Antony Worral Thompson's Slow-cooked Roast Pork Belly (Page 149) or Field Marshal Sir John Chapple's Roast Gammon (Page 155).

'There is one thing more
exasperating than a wife who
can cook and won't,
and that's a wife who can't
cook and will.'
Robert Frost

Prue Leith OBE
CHEF AND RESTAURATEUR

Grilled Tuna Steak

4 x 6 oz (150g) tuna steaks
500g fresh green beans
4 heads of bok choy (pak choi) or 250g spinach

For the dressing:
100ml soy sauce
100ml sesame oil
1 tablespoon sesame seeds

For the garnish:
8 spring onions, chopped
Handful of fresh coriander, roughly chopped
Half a red chilli, seeded and chopped

1. Prepare the dressing by mixing the soy sauce and oil together.
2. Prepare the greens by top and tailing the beans and splitting the bok choy lengthwise (or destalking and washing the spinach if bought loose – don't bother if in a packet). In separate pans of boiling water cook the beans and bok choy (or spinach) until just *al dente*, then submerge in cold water to stop cooking.
3. Heat a char-grill, griddle or frying pan. (non-stick is easiest, but doesn't make nice stripes!)   Brush with oil.
4. Turn the tuna carefully in the dressing and sprinkle with sesame seeds. Char the tuna on the hot grill or pan, turning quickly to sear the outside without cooking the middle – it should just be warmed through, but raw.
5. Reheat the greens by dunking them briefly in boiling water again, or give them a quick blast in the microwave, or toss in a wok.
6. Pile the greens on each plate, top with the tuna, sprinkle over the rest of the dressing and finish with the chopped garnish.

SERVES 4

Viscount Linley
FURNITURE DESIGNER

Slow-Cooked Game Casserole

This is a delicious recipe that must be slow-cooked to make the meat as tender and flavoursome as possible. You can vary the quantities to suit your personal taste.

Pheasant, duck, teal and partridge
A large onion
Garlic cloves
Carrots
Butter
Red wine
Vegetable stock
Bay leaves
Herbes de Provence
Salt and pepper

1. Breast and de-bone a mixture of pheasant, duck, teal and partridge, cutting the meat into reasonable chunks.
2. Seal the meat in hot butter, set aside and then gently soften the onion, garlic and carrots in the same pan, adding more butter if necessary.
3. Put all the ingredients into a large casserole, add red wine, vegetable stock and a little water to cover, bay leaves, herbes de Provence and seasoning.
4. Cover, put in the low oven of an Aga and cook overnight or cook 160C/325F/Gas mark 3 for at least 2 hours or until tender.

Delicious served with thyme-infused dumplings with redcurrant jelly on the side.

'**Cookery has become a noble art, a noble science; cooks are gentlemen.**'
Robert Burton

Jackie Llewelyn-Bowen
TV PERSONALITY

Congolese Chilli Peanut Chicken

This is a version of a dish my mother used to make when we were small and we lived in the Congo in Africa.   It's based on a Congolese dish called *'Moambe'*. This is so easy to make, so delicious and if you're a fan of chicken satay, you HAVE to try this.

2 small or 1 large onion
1 large chilli (more if you like it HOT)
2–3 cloves garlic
Dash sunflower or other unflavoured vegetable oil
6–7 pieces of chicken on the bone
1½ pints of stock, fresh or cube mixed with boiling water
Half tube or big small tin of tomato purée
3 bay leaves

1. Gently soften the finely chopped onion and one chopped red chilli (without the seeds) in a heavy pan with the finely chopped garlic in the oil, without browning. Traditionally this dish is made with palm oil, but since it's so bad for you, I've adapted this element! Depending on the heat of your chilli, add more or less.
2. Add 6–7 chicken pieces on the bone – a couple of part-boned breasts, the thighs and drumsticks, and brown the skin off gently. When you've done this take the large jug of stock and mix with 2 jars of crunchy peanut butter and a big hefty dollop of tomato purée.
3. Once the liquids are combined, add to the chicken with 3 bay leaves. Bring the heat up gently to a slow simmer and then turn the heat right down.
4. Simmer gently for 25–30 minutes or until the chicken is cooked through, checking regularly that the heat is not too hot. The peanut sauce will burn easily if you're trying to cook it too fast. Add more stock if you need to maintain the required consistency. The sauce should be rich, thick and gooey but still liquid. If you're being posh, you can toast or grill some crushed peanuts to sprinkle over the top just before you serve this. Serve with rice studded with lots of fresh parsley and a crisp green salad. Yum, now I'm starving hungry!

SERVES 4–5

Giorgio Locatelli
CHEF AND RESTAURATEUR

Coniglio Al Forno Con Prosciutto Crudo e Polenta

Rabbit with Parma Ham and Polenta

6 rabbit legs, boned
12 thin slices of Parma ham
2 tbsp groundnut oil
50g/2 oz butter
500g/1lb 2oz lard, melted
125g/4 oz polenta
1.2 litres/2 pints milk
2 heads of radicchio trevisano
Sea salt and freshly ground black pepper

1. Wrap each rabbit leg in 2 slices of Parma ham. Heat half the oil in a large, shallow casserole and place the rabbit legs in it.
2. Fry over a medium heat until they start to colour then add the butter. Turn the legs over and cook for a further 2 minutes.
3. Cover the legs completely with the melted lard then cover with foil and cook very gently in the oven for 1 hour at 120C/250F/Gas mark ½ until very tender.
4. Meanwhile cook the polenta. Put it in a large jug so that it can be poured in a steady stream.
5. Bring the milk to the boil in a large saucepan; it should half fill the pan. Add 1 teaspoon of salt and then slowly add the polenta in a continuous stream, stirring with a long-handled whisk all the time, until completely blended. The polenta will start to bubble volcanically. Reduce the heat as low as possible and cook for 20 minutes, stirring occasionally.
6. Cut each radicchio into 3 and season with salt and pepper. Brush with the remaining oil and cook on a medium-hot griddle pan until wilted. Spoon the polenta on to 6 serving plates and put the rabbit legs on top. Add the radicchio to the side and serve straight away.

SERVES 6

Recipe taken from *Tony & Giorgio* (Fourth Estate) text © Tony Allan and Giorgio Locatelli 2003.
Photographs © Jason Lowe 2003

Dame Vera Lynn DBE

SINGER AND FORCES' SWEETHEART

Chicken in the Pot

1 whole chicken
2 carrots
1 parsnip
1 stick celery
1 leek
1 onion
2 cloves garlic
2 bay leaves
1 chicken stock cube in water
Salt and pepper
Parsley, chopped

1. Cut the chicken into portions, wash well and take off skin for healthy eating.
2. Place in a large pot, cover well with cold water, bring to the boil and skim if necessary.
3. Add all the vegetables, chopped, bay leaves and chicken stock. Season with salt and pepper.
4. Cook on medium heat for at least 1–1½ hours.
5. Garnish with chopped parsley and serve with vermicelli.

SERVES 6

'Herbs are used for two purposes a. to add a flavour that isn't there but should have been and b. to take away a flavour that is there that shouldn't have been.'
William Rushton,
'The Alternative Gardener.'

Dame Vera Lynn DBE
SINGER AND FORCES' SWEETHEART

Chicken or Turkey Boobs

2 chicken or turkey breasts
1 large onion, sliced
1 garlic, chopped
1–2 tomatoes, chopped
6–8 small mushrooms, finely sliced
Stock
Herbs
Olive oil

1. Saute the onion and garlic in the hot oil then add the chicken breasts and brown on each side.
2. Add the chopped tomatoes and sliced mushrooms then a little stock to make a sauce.
3. Cover and simmer until the chicken is tender.
4. Add herbs and serve.

SERVES 2

'Strange to see how a good
dinner and feasting
reconciles everybody.'
Samuel Pepys

Claire Macdonald
CHEF AND HOTELIER

Pork Fillets with Apples, Onions, Cider and Cream

2¾ lb/1.25kg pork fillet, trimmed of membrane and cut into neat
 finger-thick strips
Milk (sufficient to cover the meat in the marinating dish)
3 tbsp olive oil
2 onions, skinned and thinly sliced
4 apples, peeled, cored, sliced and brushed with 2 tbsp
 lemon juice
1 pint/600ml dry cider
½ pt/300ml double cream
Sea salt
Freshly ground black pepper
A grating of nutmeg

1. Put the pork fillet into a dish and cover it with milk. Leave it to marinate for at least 2 hours – or overnight.
2. Heat the olive oil in a large sauté pan and cook the onions until they are soft and just beginning to colour.
3. Scoop them into a warm bowl, and then brown the pork fillet, in relays. Put them into the bowl with the onions.
4. Put the sliced apples into the sauté pan with the cider, and simmer gently until the cider has reduced by about a third, and the apples are soft.
5. Carefully – so as not to break the apple slices – replace the pork and the onions in the sauté pan and stir them into the cider and apples.
6. Add the cream and season with salt, pepper and nutmeg.
Let the cream bubble for a few minutes, which will slightly thicken the sauce and at the same time reheat the pork and onions.

Serve with red cabbage, if you like.

SERVES 6

Nick Mason
DRUMMER – PINK FLOYD

Bouillabaisse

1.5 lbs monkfish
1 lb mackerel
1 generous litre fish stock made with mackerel after filleting.
    Cover head and tail of mackerel with 1 litre water and bring to
    boil. Simmer 15 minutes. Strain and reserve the stock.
1 large crab, ask fishmonger to crack it and prepare it
4 fl oz olive oil
1 medium onion, sliced
1 leek, sliced
1 celery stalk, sliced
1 large tomato, peeled, seeded and chopped,
3 cloves garlic, chopped
1 bouquet garni
Strip of orange peel
½ chopped fennel bulb (bulb is best but could use some fronds)
¼ teaspoon saffron
½ cup chopped parsley
Seasoning
Tomato paste
Pernod
Croutons
Gruyere

1. Heat oil in large pot and stir in onions, celery and leeks to sweat.
2. Add stock, tomato, bouquet garni, garlic, orange peel and fennel.
3. Sprinkle in saffron and seasoning and simmer for 40 minutes.
4. Now make the rouille – see below
5. Add the mackerel and crab to the vegetable mix and boil hard
for 7 minutes.
6. Don't stir and disturb but shake occasionally.
7. Lay white fish on top and boil for 15 minutes more. The rolling
boil will emulsify the oil.
8. Remove fish and whisk in tomato paste and Pernod.
9. Return fish and sprinkle parsley on top.
10. Serve the bouillabaisse with croutons of toasted French bread,
Gruyere and rouille

Rouille:
1 slice de-crusted bread
2 tbsp water
1 chilli pepper
1 egg yolk
3–4 cloves garlic
4 fl oz olive oil
Seasoning

1. Soak the bread in 2 tablespoons water. Squeeze dry.
2. Purée the bread with the chilli, garlic, egg yolk, salt and 2 tablespoons oil.
3. With the blender running, trickle in the remaining oil (as for mayonnaise).

James May

TV PRESENTER AND JOURNALIST

Fish Pie

Piece of filleted cod
Piece of filleted smoked haddock
Peeled prawns
Peas
Mushrooms
Capers from the door of the fridge
Potatoes for mashing
Salt
Milk
Knob of butter
Flour
Water

Tools:
Cooker
Large saucepan
Another smaller saucepan
Large shallow frying pan
Pie dish
Potato peeler
Potato masher
Knife
Spatula
Plates, knives and forks

1. Put the water in the large saucepan with a pinch of salt. Set it on the cooker to boil. While this is happening, peel the potatoes with the potato peeler and cut them into roughly equal bits about the size of a piece of cheese. When the water is boiling, put the potatoes in it.
2. Meanwhile, put the milk in the shallow frying pan and set it on a low heat. You should not let it boil over, but it will. When it is simmering, put the fish fillets in so the milk covers them.
3. The potatoes are ready when your knife just goes into them with no real resistance. The fish is ready when it becomes opaque and flakes easily from its skin. Flake the fish into the pie dish and add the prawns, capers and chopped mushrooms. Save the fishy milk. Drain the potatoes, retrieve them from the plug hole, and put them to one side.
4. Put a knob of butter in the other smaller saucepan and melt it over some heat. Gradually stir in flour until you don't quite have a ball, but almost do. Slowly add the fishy milk, stirring like a b*****d otherwise it sticks to the pan. It will form a sauce the consistency of school custard. Pour this all over the stuff in the pie dish.
5. Mash the potatoes with the potato masher, adding milk and/or butter for richness. Spread this evenly over the top of the pie dish with the spatula. Finally, use the peas to spell a rude word on the top. Put in the oven on about 190C/375F/Gas mark 5 for a bit.

Serve on plates with knives and forks.

The Hon. Mrs David McAlpine

ACTRESS (ANGHARAD REES) AND JEWELLERY DESIGNER

My Boys' Rice Dish

A little background to this creation: both my sons Linford and Rhys, for moral reasons, chose to become vegetarians at ages 13 and 11 and this posed some problems for their adoring mother to ensure they had a very nutritional diet at an age when good nourishment is crucial. The combination of the ingredients in this recipe provides first class protein, minerals, vitamins and "good" carbohydrate. I prefer to use organic ingredients and will go to great lengths to find them.

> Short grain organic brown rice
> Cannellini beans
> Spring onions
> Masses and masses of fresh coriander
> Sesame seeds
> Pine kernels
> Sunflower seeds
> Poppy seeds
> Pumpkin seeds
> Tamari Sauce (Japanese soy sauce)
> A lot of fresh garlic cloves
> Sea salt and freshly ground black pepper

1. Cook the rice carefully according to the instructions on the packet. It should be *al dente*.
2. Cook the cannellini beans which have soaked overnight (you can use tins but drain and wash very carefully).
3. Crush garlic and chop coriander finely.
4. Mix all the ingredients together in a big bowl and check seasoning. Be liberal with seeds.

I think this is perfect as it is but tofu can be added and if the vegetarian allows, prawns can be added too.

103

Sister Mericia Pestana
THE FRANCISCAN SISTERS OF OUR LADY OF VICTORIES

Hotpot

This is Sister Mericia's recipe which she cooks for the Chelsea Pensioners in Clergy House after their annual Maundy Thursday visit to Westminster Cathedral when 12 Catholic Pensioners become an integral part of the Evening Mass of the Lord's Supper officiated by the Cardinal, the Archbishop of Westminster. Halfway through the service the Pensioners come to the front, each with a bare right foot. The Cardinal then works his way along the row, gently washing and drying each man's foot, with great humility.

600g stewing meat, diced and tossed in flour, salt and pepper
Four large potatoes, sliced
Two large onions, sliced
200g mushrooms
Mixed vegetables – carrots, peas, celery – diced
One pack (43g) of Schwartz beef casserole mix made up according
    to packet instructions – alternatively use homemade stock
Vegetable oil

1. In a non-stick frying pan fry the onions in a tablespoon of oil until translucent. Set to one side.
2. Fry the mushrooms. Set to one side.
3. In the same pan add a little more oil and brown the diced seasoned meat. Stir.
4. In a Pyrex dish layer up the ingredients, a layer of onion, then sliced potato, then vegetables – celery, carrots, peas etc to taste - and then a layer of meat and mushrooms.
Continue layering until all the ingredients are used up, ending with a layer of sliced potato.
5. Pour over the stock, shaking the dish a little to ensure it seeps down through the layers.
6. Cover the dish with foil and place in a slow oven 160C/325F/Gas mark 3 for at least two and a half hours. If the dish is not browned, remove the foil towards the end of the cooking time so that the hotpot has a nice golden colour. Enjoy!

SERVES 4

Anton Mosimann OBE
CHEF AND RESTAURATEUR

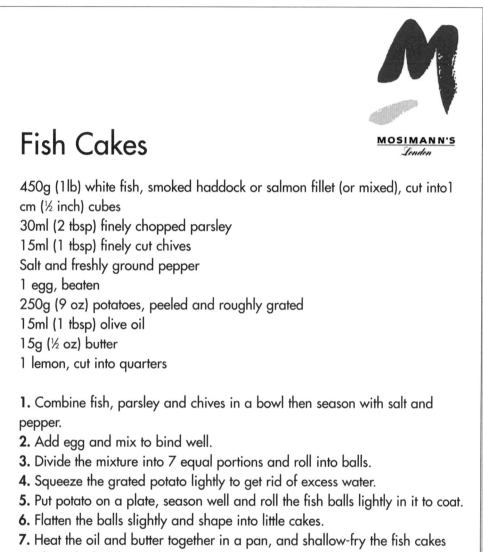

Fish Cakes

450g (1lb) white fish, smoked haddock or salmon fillet (or mixed), cut into1 cm (½ inch) cubes
30ml (2 tbsp) finely chopped parsley
15ml (1 tbsp) finely cut chives
Salt and freshly ground pepper
1 egg, beaten
250g (9 oz) potatoes, peeled and roughly grated
15ml (1 tbsp) olive oil
15g (½ oz) butter
1 lemon, cut into quarters

1. Combine fish, parsley and chives in a bowl then season with salt and pepper.
2. Add egg and mix to bind well.
3. Divide the mixture into 7 equal portions and roll into balls.
4. Squeeze the grated potato lightly to get rid of excess water.
5. Put potato on a plate, season well and roll the fish balls lightly in it to coat.
6. Flatten the balls slightly and shape into little cakes.
7. Heat the oil and butter together in a pan, and shallow-fry the fish cakes gently on both sides until crisp and golden brown in colour (about 6–7 minutes).
8. Drain well on kitchen paper.
9. Serve with the lemon quarters for squeezing over the fish cakes.

SERVES 4

Jamie Oliver
CHEF AND RESTAURATEUR

Honeymoon Spaghetti

I first tried this at Hotel St Pietro in Positano, Italy, where Jools and I stayed for a week of our honeymoon. You will need a piece of baking parchment measuring 60 x 120 cm/ 2 x 4 ft to make a large cooking parcel. The steam will cause the 'parcel' to puff up in the oven, which looks good at the table if you serve it straight away.

1 x 1.5kg/3½ lb crab or lobster
2 cloves of garlic, chopped
1 fresh red chilli, deseeded and finely sliced
30g/1 oz butter
1 tbsp olive oil
170g/6 oz shelled tiger or small prawns
455g/1 lb live mussels, cleaned
115g/4 oz squid, sliced
455g/1 lb spaghetti, cooked al dente
1 handful of flat leaf parsley and marjoram, roughly chopped
1 egg, beaten

For the sauce:
1 tbsp olive oil
3 cloves of garlic, roughly chopped
1 fresh red chilli, finely chopped
2 x 400g/14 oz tins of plum tomatoes
Sea salt and freshly ground black pepper

1. Preheat the oven to 180C/350F/Gas mark 4.
2. Plunge the crab or lobster into boiling water, boil for 15 minutes, then remove.
3. When cooled, remove all the meat from the shell, flaking it up into small pieces and removing any splinters of shell.
4. To make the sauce, fry the empty shell and legs in the olive oil with the garlic and chilli.
5. Using the end of a rolling pin, pound up the shells, add the tomatoes and a large glass of water and simmer for 1 hour. Pass through a sieve, season to taste and put aside.
6. In a large pan gently fry the garlic and chilli (from the main ingredients list) in the butter and olive oil. Turn the heat up and add the mussels, squid and prawns. Cook for 2 minutes, remove

from the heat and discard any unopened mussels.

7. Add the tomato sauce, cooked spaghetti, lobster or crab meat and herbs and mix together.

8. Fold the parchment in half to get a crease and open it out again. Place the seafood mixture in the centre of one half and brush all the edges with egg. Bring the two sides together and seal well. Carefully slide the parcel onto a baking tray and cook for about 10 minutes until puffed up. Serve straight away.

SERVES 4

Happy Days with the Naked Chef by Jamie Oliver (Michael Joseph 2001) Copyright (©) Jamie Oliver 2001. Photograph copyright © David Loftus 2001.

Photograph courtesy of David Loftus

Tom Parker Bowles
FOOD COLUMNIST

Chicken and Mushroom Pie

1 cold roast chicken, flesh stripped
80g unsalted butter
80g plain flour
1 pint chicken stock
Glass of dry white wine
1 lemon, juiced
Big glug Tabasco
1 large onion, finely chopped
225g fresh mushrooms, sliced (field mushrooms or ceps, in season)
Handful dried morel, soaked in warm water (optional)
Handful of chopped tarragon and parsley
Sea salt and fresh pepper
1 pack of good puff pastry (look for the one made with butter
    rather than vegetable oil)
1 egg, beaten, for glaze

1. Make roux by melting butter gently, stirring in flour and cooking it out for about 5 minutes. Then whisk in hot stock until you have a thick sauce and season.
2. Add mustard, lemon juice and Tabasco and cook gently for further 2 minutes.
3. Sauté onions until soft then add mushrooms and cook for a further few minutes. Increase heat; add wine and burn off all the booze. Bring to the boil and add to sauce, stirring and cooking for a minute more.
4. Add chicken and herbs to sauce and allow to cool.
5. Preheat oven to 200C/400F/Gas mark 6. Put chicken mix into pie dish and top with pastry. Use an upturned egg-cup or pie bird to support the pastry in the middle, crimp the edges and cut a X in the middle.
6. Brush with beaten egg and bake for 30 minutes or until golden.

SERVES 4

The Phoenix
GASTRO PUB, LONDON SW3

Butter Poached Chicken Breast, Saffron Risotto, Chorizo Dumpling, and Pumpkin Purée

Here is a wonderful recipe from our amazing Head Chef Drew King which our regular Chelsea Pensioners will love.

5 corn fed chicken breasts
Risotto rice
4 shallots
2 litres hot chicken stock
Pinch saffron
1 clove garlic
1 butternut squash
200g cubed chorizo
Deep fried sage leaves
150g butter
100ml double cream
1 egg
1 tbsp of crème fraiche
100g grated Parmesan

1. *For the risotto* – add diced shallots and garlic to a medium hot pan, sweat off in butter and add risotto rice. Sweat the rice to open the pores of the rice. Add the saffron and the remaining stock, bit by bit, until the risotto is *al dente*. Set aside and chill.
2. *For the dumpling* – blitz 1 chicken breast in a processor. Add the double cream and the egg and season generously. Fold the chorizo into this mixture. Wrap in cling film and tie off into golf ball sizes, tying and sealing the cling film to make water tight. Set aside.
3. *For the purée* – dice the squash, place in a pan and cover with water. Season. Cook until soft. Take out and blitz, adding a knob of butter and touch of cream. Season again to taste. Set aside.
4. *For the chicken* – season and seal the chicken breasts, skin side down, in a searing hot pan with olive oil until they are golden brown, then do the same with the under sides. Put 1 litre of stock into the same pan and add the butter. Poach the chicken on low

heat for about 10 minutes, covered in foil.

5. Poach the dumplings until cooked through in simmering water for 8 minutes.

6. While this is cooking, finish the risotto – reapply to the heat and add the crème fraiche and Parmesan and fold through. Check the chicken breasts are hot.

7. Then put the dish together – the chicken breast to the left of the plate on a bed of the risotto, the dumpling to the right of the plate, slashes of the purée down the middle, garnished with the sage leaves at the top of the plate.

SERVES 4

Rt. Hon. Michael Portillo
JOURNALIST AND POLITICIAN

Tabouleh Salad

This light and refreshing Middle Eastern salad, an excellent alternative to rice or pasta, is good made the day before it is eaten, but don't add the tomatoes until you are ready to serve it.

8 oz/250g cous cous or bulgur wheat
14 fl oz/400ml boiling stock, vegetable or chicken
3 spring onions
4 tomatoes, skinned and chopped
2 tbsp chopped parsley
2 tbsp chopped mint
2 tbsp lemon juice
4 tbsp olive oil
Salt and freshly ground black pepper

1. Put the cous cous and salt in a bowl, pour over the boiling stock and leave for 15–20 minutes or until the stock has been absorbed and the cous cous softened.

2. Add the remaining ingredients and mix carefully together.

SERVES 6–8

111

Gordon Ramsay
CHEF AND RESTAURATEUR

Duck Breasts with Blackcurrant Sauce and Gratin Dauphinoise

'Duck breasts are fantastic paired with a blackcurrant sauce which helps to cut through the richness of the meat. When in season, add some fresh blackcurrants to the sauce. Serve with buttered green beans or a side salad for a balanced meal.'

4 duck breasts, with skin on
Sea salt and freshly ground black pepper

Gratin Dauphinoise:
200ml whole milk
200ml double cream
1 bay leaf
1 garlic clove, peeled and lightly crushed
1kg waxy potatoes (Desirée or Charlotte)
200g grated medium cheddar
Sea salt and freshly ground black pepper
Olive oil, to drizzle

Blackcurrant sauce:
300ml dry red wine
2 garlic cloves, skin on and lightly crushed
Few sprigs of thyme
300ml duck (or brown chicken) stock
4-5 tbsp blackcurrant jam or conserve
30g butter, cut into cubes

1. Prepare the Gratin Dauphinoise. Preheat oven to 200C/Fan 180/Gas mark 6. Lightly oil a deep gratin dish. Put the milk, cream, bay leaf and garlic in a pan; heat until simmering. When the liquid begins to bubble up the sides of the pan, turn off heat and leave to cool slightly.
2. Peel and finely slice the potatoes using a mandolin. Spread a third of the cheese on the bottom of a baking dish and cover with a layer of the potatoes, overlapping the sides. Season each layer as you go along. Repeat layering the cheese and potatoes until you've used up the ingredients, finishing with a layer of cheese. Strain the

creamy milk and discard the bay leaf and garlic. Pour the mixture over the potatoes until it comes two-thirds up the sides. (You may not need all of it.) Gently press down on the potatoes to help the liquid absorb; sprinkle with a little more cheese.

3. Bake in the oven for 30-40 minutes or until the potatoes are golden brown and tender when prodded with a sharp knife. Leave to cool for a few minutes before serving.

4. Score the skin of the duck breasts in a crisscross pattern, then rub with salt and pepper. Place them, skin-side down, on a dry ovenproof pan and cook over very low heat to render down most of the fat. This may take 10-15 minutes.

5. For the sauce, place the red wine in a pan with the garlic and thyme and boil until reduced by half. Pour in the stock and reduce again by half. Stir the blackcurrant jam into the sauce and add a few knobs of butter to give it a shine. Taste and adjust the seasoning, then strain through a fine sieve and discard the solids.

6. Turn up the heat for the duck breasts and fry until the skin is crisp. Turn them over and cook the other side for 1–2 minutes. Place the pan into the hot oven for 8-10 minutes for medium. The duck should be slightly springy when pressed.

7. Rest the duck breasts on a warm plate for 5 minutes, then slice into halves on the diagonal. Place on to warmed serving plates. Spoon over the blackcurrant sauce; serve with a portion of gratin Dauphinoise.

SERVES 4

'Food without wine is a corpse; wine without food is a ghost; united and well matched they are as body and soul, living partners.'
André Simon

113

Paul Rankin
CHEF AND RESTAURATEUR

Salad of Crispy Duck – with Mango, Ginger and Chilli

4 female duck legs
1 bulb garlic
I knob ginger
Coriander leaves
1 tbsp rock salt
4 tbsp black peppercorns
1 mango
1 bulb coriander
1 red chilli
1 bottle of rice vinegar (500mls)
10g dried chilli flakes
500g caster sugar
6 limes juiced
Asian shallots
2 baby gem lettuce
1 tin or jar duck fat
300mls fish sauce

1. Duck Legs. Firstly marinade the duck legs. Place in a tray and cover with salt, garlic, black peppercorns and coriander leaves. Leave in the fridge to marinade overnight.
The next day wipe off marinade, place in duck fat and confit (cook slowly) in the oven for approx 1½–2 hours at 160C/325F/Gas mark 3.
2. Dressing. Mix the dried chilli flakes, rice vinegar, fish sauce, sugar and lime juice together and dissolve the sugar over a moderate heat then set aside.
3. Salad. Wash baby gems and spin dry, mix with slices of mango, chilli, coriander leaves and Asian shallots and peanuts.
4. To Serve. Toss the salad lightly in the dressing, crisp the duck legs up under the grill or in the oven, skin side down until warm and crisp. Take the bone out of the leg by twisting, slice and serve hot on top of the salad. Sprinkle some toasted peanuts on for garnish.

SERVES 4

Sir Steve Redgrave CBE

OLYMPIC OARSMAN

Baked Penne with Dolcelatte Cheese and Radicchio

250g penne rigate
50g butter
250g butter mushrooms, sliced
2 garlic cloves, chopped finely
15ml spoon finely chopped fresh sage
1 small head of radicchio (250–275g), cored and shredded finely
250ml double cream or crème fraiche
50g Parmesan cheese, finely grated
175g Dolcelatte cheese, cubed
Salt and freshly ground black pepper
Fresh sage leaves, to garnish

1. Preheat the oven to 230C/ 450F/ Gas mark 8 and butter a 23 x 28cm ovenproof dish.
2. Melt the butter in a large frying pan and fry the mushrooms and garlic for about 5 minutes until softened.
3. Stir in the sage and radicchio and remove the pan from the heat.
4. In a large bowl stir together the cream, Parmesan and Dolcelatte.
5. Add the mushroom mixture and pasta cooked according to instructions. Taste and adjust the seasoning.
6. Transfer the mixture to the ovenproof dish and bake in the oven for 12–15 minutes, or until the top is browned and bubbly.

SERVES 4

Ruth Rogers
CHEF AND RESTAURATEUR

Green Bean and Tomato Tagliatelle

This is a summer pasta. Always use the ripest tomatoes and the finest green beans.

16 oz egg tagliatelle
1 lb fine green beans
6 plum tomatoes
2 oz Parmesan
1 garlic clove
5 fl oz double cream
3 tbsp basil leaves

1. Top and tail the green beans, cook in boiling salted water until tender, then drain.
2. Cut the tomatoes in half, remove the juice and seeds and chop the flesh coarsely. Season.
3. Grate the Parmesan.
4. Peel the garlic, add to the cream and bring to a boil. Season.
5. Remove the garlic and add the tomato, green beans and basil.
6. Stir to combine.
7. Cook the tagliatelle in boiling salted water until *al dente*.
8. Drain and add to the tomatoes and beans. Serve with Parmesan.

SERVES 4

River Café Easy by Rose Gray and Ruth Rogers (Ebury Press 2003) Copyright (©) Rose Gray and Ruth Rogers 2003

'Tomatoes and oregano make it Italian; wine and tarragon make it French. Sour cream makes it Russian; lemon and cinnamon make it Greek. Soy sauce makes it Chinese; garlic makes it good.'
Alice May Brock

Ruth Rogers
CHEF AND RESTAURATEUR

Spaghetti, Raw Tomato and Rocket

Plum tomatoes are fleshy, easy to peel and have hardly any juice or seeds, which makes them ideal for making rich, thick tomato sauces. This raw sauce should only be made in the summer, when you can buy sun-ripened plum tomatoes that are really sweet.

320g spaghetti
4 plum tomatoes
2 garlic cloves
1 dried chilli
2 tbsp capers
3 tbsp black olives
3 tbsp rocket leaves
3 tbsp extra virgin olive oil

1. Cut the tomatoes in half. Squeeze out excess juice and seeds and chop the flesh coarsely.
2. Peel the garlic and squash with 1 teaspoon of sea salt.
3. Crumble the chilli, rinse the capers and stone the olives.
4. Roughly chop the rocket.
5. Combine the tomatoes with all the ingredients except for the rocket. Season generously, add the olive oil and put aside for 30 minutes.
6. Cook the spaghetti in boiling salted water until *al dente*. Drain and stir the pasta into the tomatoes.
7. Add the rocket and toss to coat each strand. Season with black pepper.
Serve with olive oil.

SERVES 4

Michel Roux

CHEF AND RESTAURATEUR

Oeufs à *la* Tripe

3 onions
4 eggs hard-boiled
500ml milk
1 heaped tablespoon plain flour
1 tablespoon butter
Salt, pepper, nutmeg
100g grated Gruyere, Emmental
Olive oil

1. Peel and cut the onions in half then slice, cook in a little olive oil until lightly browned and tender then drain on kitchen cloth.
2. Make a Roux with the butter and flour and pour the milk onto this, whisk well and cook to make a white sauce. Season well with salt, pepper and nutmeg.
3. Cut the eggs in half and place yolk side down in a buttered ovenproof dish.
4. Scatter the onions onto the eggs and then pour the sauce over.
5. Finally sprinkle the cheese on top then bake in a medium oven until hot and golden brown.

SERVES 4

A Life in the Kitchen by Michel Roux (Weidenfeld & Nicolson, The Orion Publishing Group 2009) © Michel Roux 2009. Photograph © Cristian Barnett

'Anybody can make you enjoy the first bite of a dish, but only a real chef can make you enjoy the last.'
Francois Minot

The Marquess of Salisbury PC DL
CHAIRMAN OF THE CHELSEA PENSIONERS' APPEAL

Loin of Venison with Green Pepper Sauce

2 whole venison loins

For the marinade:
½ bottle red wine
1 carrot, chopped
1 onion, chopped
2 garlic cloves, crushed
1 celery stick, chopped
4 juniper berries
Bay leaf
Small bunch of thyme

For the sauce:
½ onion, chopped
1 tablespoon green peppercorns (in brine), chopped
½ pint beef or lamb stock
1 good tablespoon crème fraiche
Olive oil
Butter

1. To prepare the sauce, fry the onion until soft then add the peppercorns and stock. Bring to the boil and reduce by half.
Add a good tablespoon of crème fraiche.
2. Dry the venison and season with salt. Heat a knob of butter and some olive oil in a frying pan then fry the meat on all sides, for no longer than one minute.
3. Place meat in the oven at 180C/350F/Gas mark 4 for 5–10 minutes (for medium to rare).
4. Deglaze the frying pan and add the juices to the sauce.
5. Remove meat from the oven and allow to rest for 10 minutes.
Slice as thinly as possible and serve on a hot plate with game chips and braised red cabbage.
Serve the sauce separately.

SERVES 4

Prunella Scales CBE

ACTRESS

Coq au Vin

1 tablespoon butter
1 tablespoon oil
4 large chicken joints
1 small piece (say 6oz) unsmoked streaky bacon
16 button onions
2 garlic cloves, crushed
2 sprigs fresh thyme
2 bay leaves
1 bottle ordinary red wine
6-8 dark-gilled mushrooms
1 rounded tablespoon butter
1 tablespoon flour
Salt and ground black pepper

1. Heat the oil and butter in a heavy-based frying pan and fry the chicken joints, skin side down, until nicely golden. Turn them over and do the other side then place in the cooking pot.
2. Brown the onions a little and add them to the pot.
3. Put the crushed garlic and sprigs of thyme and bay leaves in amongst the chicken pieces. Season with salt and pepper.
4. Pour in the wine, cover the pan and simmer gently until the meat is tender.
5. During the last 15 minutes of cooking, add the mushrooms and stir them in.
6. Remove the chicken, bacon, onions and mushrooms and place on a warm serving dish.
7. Discard the bay leaves and thyme and bring the liquid to a fast boil to reduce it by about one third.
8. Mix the flour and butter into a paste, add it to the liquid and bring back to the boil, whisking all the time until the sauce has thickened. Pour it over the chicken pieces.

SERVES 4

Alexandra Shulman
EDITOR UK VOGUE

Pasta with Broccoli and Chilli

2 large heads broccoli
1 small red chilli
2 large cloves garlic
500g penne or rigatoni
150g pine nuts
Parmesan
4tbsp olive oil
Salt
Pepper

1. Separate the broccoli florets and steam so that they have just started to be cooked – about 5 minutes over boiling water.
2. Put a large pan of water on for the pasta.
3. Heat the olive oil in another pan to medium, and very finely chop the garlic and chilli and add – don't let them burn. How much of the chilli you put in depends on how hot you like things.
4. Put in the steamed broccoli and stir while you boil the pasta. You can smash it around a bit so the pieces aren't too big.
5. Crush the pine nuts in a food processor or pestle and mortar so that they are like large crumbs rather than dust. Throw them into the broccoli mixture and grate as much cheese as you like on top.
6. Mix it all in. Add salt and pepper to taste.
The more cheese you add, the less salt you will need.
7. Drain pasta and add the broccoli with a little bit of the pasta water, just to help mix it in.

If you like it really salty you can add five chopped tinned anchovy fillets to the olive oil, garlic and chilli at the start.

SERVES A GENEROUS 4

'Cooking is like love, it
should be entered into with
abandon or not at all.'
Harriet Van Horne, **Vogue**

Wayne Sleep OBE
DANCER

Paella

Having lived with José for 14 years I've never had to cook this dish. My only participation is to decant the wine – my normal contribution to dinner. However I've often watched him make this very delicious seafood paella, which he does creatively and spontaneously, with no specific instructions or definite quantities.

1 large onion
1 red pepper
Saffron strands – for colour and flavour – soaked in a little water
3 cloves garlic
3 bay leaves
Salt and pepper
Olive oil
1 squid
Fillet of cod
Fillet of haddock
Mussels
Clams
Small prawns
6 tiger prawns
Risotto rice – 6 cups (or handfuls as José would say)
White wine
Boiling water
1 lemon

1. Cut the squid into pieces and fry in some hot olive oil.
2. Add the wine, salt and pepper and cook until the wine has reduced – then put aside.
3. Chop the onion, red pepper and garlic into small pieces then add to some hot oil in a paella dish, wok or frying pan. Stir and season with salt and pepper.
4. When cooked *al dente*, add the chopped cod and haddock and stir together.
5. After a few minutes, when the fish is cooked, add the rice, bay leaves, soaked saffron and its liquid. Stir until the rice is coated.
6. Add 3 cups of boiling water (use twice as much in volume as the rice you have used) and stir until the rice has been cooking for 10 minutes. Then add the clams and mussels.

7. It is important that you never stir the mixture after adding the clams and mussels – only shake the pan – this is one of the reasons why a paella dish has handles.

8. Just before the rice is cooked add the prawns and the squid to the top of the dish.

9. When cooked, turn off the heat and cover the dish with a cloth. Squeeze over the juice of the lemon when you are ready to eat.

SERVES 4–6

Mark Johnson
HEAD CHEF – THE SLOANE CLUB, CHELSEA

Steak, Guinness and Mushroom Pie

1 kg diced beef featherblade
400g button mushrooms
200g sliced onions
1 bottle Guinness
1 tbsp tomato purée
2 tbsp plain flour
2 pts chicken stock
1 tbsp Worcestershire Sauce
Salt and pepper
Organic puff pastry
1 egg
Drop of water

1. Season the beef and sauté until well coloured.
2. Add the onions and mushrooms and brown in the same pan.
3. Add the Guinness and reduce to a syrup.
4. Add the tomato purée, flour, chicken stock and Worcestershire Sauce.
5. Cook slowly for 2 hours until tender.
6. Put into pie dishes and chill.
7. Cover with organic puff pastry and brush with egg wash.
8. Cook for 35 minutes at 180C/350F/Gas mark 4 until golden.

MAKES 1 LARGE PIE OR 6 INDIVIDUAL PIES.

'He who eats alone chokes
alone.'
Proverb

Alexis Soyer 1810 – 1858

At the time of the Crimean War the military catering was so bad that the food killed more soldiers than the enemy did. One person who improved the situation considerably was Alexis Soyer, a French-born chef who had made his reputation as the *'chef de cuisine'* in 1837 at London's Reform Club. Soyer spontaneously invented Lamb Cutlets Reform when a cantankerous and hungry member of the club arrived late for dinner and Soyer had to make the most of what was in his kitchen. His 19th Century classic is still on the menu there.

Soyer's first success at mass catering was in Ireland, during the Potato Famine in 1847 when he fed 5,000 people at one go with soup from his newly invented soup kitchen. Shortly afterwards he began to market his 'magic stove' which was portable, simple and efficient, using any available solid fuel.

Alexis Soyer and Florence Nightingale worked together to reorganise the provisions and cooking facilities in the army hospitals and the use of Soyer's cooker in trenches meant that men didn't have to risk their lives when they crawled out to find food. The Army Catering Corps wasn't founded until 1945 but Soyer laid the foundations.

Capable of boiling 12 gallons of liquid, Soyer's stoves were used almost continually by the British Army until the 1980s. Much of the stock of the stoves was lost in the sinking of the Atlantic Conveyor during the Falklands War but they were used right up until the First Gulf War.

In April 2009 HRH the Princess Royal opened Alexis Soyer House in Worthy Down, the splendid new Headquarters of the Defence Food Services School where the trainee chefs learn how to become both peacetime and combat caterers.

Lamb Cutlets Reform

There are many variations of the recipe for Lamb Cutlets Reform, some with very long lists of ingredients, but this version is less complicated than others.

900g best end neck or lamb cutlets
1 tbsp seasoned plain flour
5–6 tbsp white breadcrumbs
1 beaten egg
50g finely chopped cooked ham
4 tbsp olive oil
25g butter

For the garnish:
1 carrot, peeled and cut into short, fine strips
3 gherkins
1 egg white, steamed
3 mushrooms
2–3 tbsp beef stock
15g butter

For the sauce:
1 tsp redcurrant jelly
1 tbsp port
150ml demi-glace sauce/good stock, available in good shops
A pinch of cayenne pepper

1. Roll the cutlets in the seasoned flour.
2. Mix together the breadcrumbs and chopped ham.
3. Brush the cutlets with beaten egg and coat thoroughly in the breadcrumb mixture.

Garnish:
1. Cook the carrot in boiling water for 2–3 minutes.
2. Slice the gherkins, mushrooms and steamed egg white into small, even pieces.
3. In a frying pan heat together the stock, butter, carrot, gherkins, egg white and mushrooms for 2–3 minutes. Set aside.

Sauce:
1. Melt the redcurrant jelly with the port in a pan.
2. Add the demi-glace sauce, a pinch of cayenne, boil then set aside.

Lamb:
1. Heat the oil and butter in a large frying pan.
2. Fry the cutlets until golden, about 4 minutes on each side.

Warm through the sauce and garnish then arrange cutlets in a circle on a warmed plate, pile garnish in the centre and pour the sauce around.

SERVES 6

Rick Stein OBE

CHEF AND RESTAURATEUR

Fish Pasties with French Tarragon

Use the cheapest fish fillet you can find for this dish. Ling, coley, pollack or pouting (in that order of preference) are all fine. This is the recipe I use in our bakery and very good it is too!

150g (5 oz) leek, cut into 1 cm (½ in) dice
150g (5 oz) onion, cut into 1 cm (½ in) dice
225g (8 oz) potato, cut into 1 cm (½ in) dice
425g (15 oz) fish fillet cut into 2.5 cm (1 in) pieces
25ml (1 fl oz) white wine vinegar
25g (1 oz) butter
25g (1 oz) mature Cheddar, grated
½ teaspoon chopped fresh French tarragon
½ teaspoon freshly ground black pepper
1 teaspoon salt
900g (2 lb) flaky pastry or shortcrust pastry, chilled

Pre-heat the oven to 200C/400F/Gas mark 6.

1. Mix all the ingredients, except the pastry, in a bowl.
2. Roll out the pastry to about 5 mm (¼ in) thick. Using a pastry cutter, press out 5 x 19 cm (7½ in) discs.
3. Divide the filling between the five discs. Moisten the edges of the pastry then pinch them together to seal.
4. Crimp the edges then place on a lightly greased baking sheet and bake for 35 minutes. Serve hot or cold.

MAKES 5 PASTIES

Taste of the Sea by Rick Stein (BBC Books 1995) Copyright © Rick Stein 1995

Sir Jackie Stewart OBE
F1 WORLD CHAMPION 1969, 1971, 1973

Shepherd's Pie

50g/2 oz butter
2 onions, roughly chopped
15ml/1tbsp plain flour
250ml/8 fl oz well-flavoured lamb stock
575g/1¼ lb lean cooked lamb, minced
5ml/1tsp Worcestershire Sauce
675g/1½ lb potatoes, halved
15–30ml/1–2 tbsp milk
Pinch of grated nutmeg
Salt and pepper
Butter for greasing

Pre-heat the oven to 220C/425F/Gas mark 7

1. Melt half the butter in a saucepan and fry the onions until softened but not coloured.
2. Stir in the flour and cook gently for 1–2 minutes, stirring all the time.
3. Gradually add the stock and bring to the boil, stirring until the sauce thickens.
4. Stir in the lamb, with salt and pepper and Worcestershire Sauce to taste. Cover the pan and simmer for 30 minutes.
5. Meanwhile cook the potatoes in a saucepan of salted boiling water for about 30 minutes or until tender.
6. Drain thoroughly and mash with a potato masher, or beat them with a handheld electric whisk until smooth. Beat in the rest of the butter and the milk to make a creamy consistency. Add salt, pepper and nutmeg to taste.
7. Spoon the meat mixture into a greased pie dish or shallow oven-to-table dish. Cover with the potato, smooth the top, then flick it up into small peaks or score a pattern on the surface with a fork.
8. Bake for 10–15 minutes until browned on top. Serve at once.

SERVES 4–6

Janice Tchalenko
CERAMIC ARTIST

Smart Tart

1 packet ready-made puff pastry
2 large chopped onions
5 large or 8 medium leeks
3 eggs
10 fl oz crème fraiche
Cheese (optional)
Salt and black pepper

1. Roll out the pastry and line a 12 inch/30 cm greased flan tin. For a rustic look you can leave the edges over-hanging the sides.
2. In a frying pan sweat the finely chopped onions and leeks in a little oil or butter.
3. Beat the eggs and add crème fraiche and seasoning. If you are watching your waistline then use less crème fraiche
4. Put the onion and leek mixture into the pastry case and pour over the eggs and crème fraiche mixture.
5. Fold over the pastry flaps if you have left them and brush with milk.
6. Bake for 30–40 minutes at 190C/375F/Gas mark 5.

If you enjoy cheese with leeks you can crumble any cheese over the top of the tart before baking. Blue cheeses are particularly tasty. Serve hot or cold.

SERVES 8

'We should look for
someone to eat and drink
with before looking for
something to eat and drink.'
Epicurus

Mario Testino

PHOTOGRAPHER

Aji de Gallina
(Chicken with hot peppers Peruvian Style)

1 large chicken
10 fresh hot peppers
1 cup of oil
1 can of evaporated milk
1 loaf of bread (small)
1½ cups of ground dry cheese
½ lb onions (finely chopped)
2 lbs of potatoes
6 hard boiled eggs
1½ litres water
1 carrot
Salt and pepper

1. Cook the chicken in boiling water with 1 teaspoon of salt and the carrot until it is cooked.
2. Take the chicken out of the pan and when it has cooled down cut it into small pieces.
3. Cook the peppers without seeds for 5 minutes, drain, and grind with garlic.
4. Place a pan on the heat and add the oil. When it is hot fry the onions, garlic, hot pepper, salt and pepper, then the bread (which has been soaked in the milk and put through a blender) and then finally the chicken.
5. When everything is fried, pour in a cup of broth and add the cheese as garnish with boiled potatoes and eggs.

'At a dinner party one should eat wisely, but not too well and talk well, but not too wisely.'
W. Somerset Maugham

135

Leslie Thomas OBE
AUTHOR

Lamb Tagine with Almonds

3 lb lamb shoulder, cut into 1 inch cubes
2 large cloves of garlic, crushed
2 inch piece of fresh ginger, finely chopped
2 tsp cinnamon powder
2 tsp cumin seeds
2 pinches of saffron strands
1 large onion, finely chopped
3 oz blanched almonds, chopped
4 oz currants or raisins
4 oz butter
2 tbsp fresh mint, chopped
Salt and pepper
Water

1. Crush cumin seeds and saffron, add to cubed lamb, onion, garlic, cinnamon and ginger in a bowl and leave for 1 hour.
2. Preheat oven to 150C/300F/Gas mark 2.
3. Place lamb and the other ingredients in a casserole dish with the almonds, butter and currants. Add water to almost cover the contents and a pinch of salt.
4. Place in the oven for 3 hours, stirring occasionally and adding a small amount of extra water, if looking dry.
5. The tagine is ready to eat when the lamb is tender and the sauce has thickened.
6. Garnish with the chopped mint and serve, traditionally, with couscous.

'A cauliflower is a cabbage
with a college education.'
Mark Twain

Alan Titchmarsh MBE DL
GARDENER AND AUTHOR

Lamb Cutlets Shrewsbury

8 lamb cutlets
½ oz veg fat
4 ozs button mushrooms
4 tbsps redcurrant jelly
2 tbsps Worcestershire Sauce
Juice of 1 lemon
1 level tbsp plain flour
¼–½ pint stock
Salt and freshly ground pepper
Pinch ground nutmeg
Chopped parsley

1. Trim excess fat from the cutlets. Heat the fat in a frying pan and brown the cutlets on both sides in the hot fat.
2. Trim and slice the mushrooms.
3. Remove the cutlets from the pan and place in a casserole dish with the mushrooms.
4. Measure the redcurrant jelly, Worcestershire Sauce and lemon juice into a saucepan. Stir over a low heat until the jelly has melted and the ingredients are blended - stirring with a whisk often helps redcurrant jelly to soften. Draw off the heat.
5. Add the flour to the hot fat remaining in the frying pan and if necessary, add extra to help absorb the flour. Stir over low heat for about 10 minutes until a golden brown. Stir in the jelly mix and then sufficient stock to make a thick gravy. Bring to the boil, stirring all the time to get a smooth gravy. Season with salt, pepper and nutmeg. Strain over the cutlets.
6. Cover and place in a moderate to slow oven 170C/325F/Gas mark 3 and cook for 1½ hours. Sprinkle with parsley and serve.

SERVES 4

from Alan Titchmarsh

John Torode

CHEF, RESTAURATEUR AND MASTER CHEF JUDGE

Braised Oxtail and Celeriac Mash

In a restaurant you would use reduced stock for braising, because you want something gelatinous to make the sauce thick and unctuous. The simplest way to get a similar effect without having to use a thick reduced sauce is to put a veal shin or even a pig's trotter into the cooking pot. The trotter can either be discarded after cooking, or take the bone out, roll the meat up in cling-film and leave it in the fridge for a while to firm it up then slice, crumb and pan fry for a supper dish.

2 oxtails cut by the butcher
50g plain flour
4 carrots
2 leeks
6 celery stalks
2 bunches of flat-leaved parsley
2 small branches of sage
About 6 tablespoons olive oil
400g thick bacon cut into big chunks
200g veal shin or one pig's trotter
1 bottle of red wine
Water
Salt and freshly ground black pepper

Preheat the oven to 190C/375F/Gas mark 5
Use a heavy-based Le Creuset casserole.

1. Trim the tails of any excess fat. Season really well with salt and pepper and dust with a little flour.
2. Tie the carrots, leeks, celery and herbs tightly in a bundle with some string.
3. Heat the oil in a big heavy pan, add the bacon, cook for two minutes then add the oxtails. Leave to sit and sizzle. Wait until they colour and are well browned all over then they will lift naturally and come away from the pan. Turn them over and cook for a further 3 minutes, making sure to move the bacon so it doesn't burn.
4. Add the bundle of vegetables and the shin or trotter. Pour in the wine and bring up to the boil to drive off the raw alcohol, then let it bubble away and evaporate for about 10 minutes or so, scraping the sticky bits of meat from the bottom of the pot.

5. At this stage you need some liquid so pour in 2 litres of water, so that it almost covers the meat. Take a double sheet of baking paper and press into the liquid. Place in the oven 3½ hours, until the liquid has reduced right down and the meat is so soft it is falling apart. Change the paper once or twice during cooking if need be.

Celeriac Mash

This restaurant version of a mashed root vegetable seems to be a little over the top but I think the vegetable deserves this great treatment. The end result is rich. Beware serving liberally as it is very rich indeed. If you want to spice it up a little add a hunk of fresh horseradish.

1 large celeriac, peeled and diced
2 large potatoes, diced and peeled
100ml milk
Cold water
100ml olive oil
Salt and pepper

1. Place the potatoes and celeriac in a heavy based pan over a medium heat with the milk, olive oil and salt and pepper. Make sure all the vegetables are covered by topping up with the water. Cook for about 15–20 minutes until all soft.
2. Drain off the liquid and reserve. Mash the celeriac and the potatoes with a fork and then add the reserved liquid to make as sloppy as you like. The sloppier the better for me, especially with the rich gravy and soft sticky meat from the oxtail.

'If more of us valued food and cheer and song above hoarded gold, it would be a merrier world.'
J.R.R. Tolkien, Lord of the Rings

Steve Trapmore MBE
OLYMPIC OARSMAN

Stopwatch Eggs with Toasted Soldiers

On the morning of the Olympic final in Beijing I was a bit tense so I did not eat my normal 5 Weetabix and 4 slices of toast and honey. I remember collecting my tray in the huge 4000 seater dining hall and collecting a small bowl of cornflakes, a single slice of toast and a yoghurt. After spreading a small amount of butter on my toast it took me 15 minutes to force half a slice down. By this time my cornflakes had turned to mush. One spoonful made my stomach turn and that was that. The yoghurt never made it out of the pot but I won a gold!

Here are the perfect boiled eggs with hard whites and runny yolks . . . this never fails.

Have the stopwatch on EXACTLY 2 minutes standby (a microwave clock will do)

1. Put the eggs in a saucepan of cold water on the hob, which must be turned up to full heat.
2. The second the eggs start boiling (and I mean the second) start the two-minute timer.
3. Keep the eggs boiling.
4. While this is going on you will need to rush around getting the bread in the toaster, buttered and sliced asap.
5. The precise moment the two-minute timer is up lift eggs out of the water as fast as possible and into awaiting egg cups.
6. As you crack open your egg with your preferred method of entry, you will realise with relish, upon dipping in the first soldier, that this great egg is a must for the even greater British Soldier!!!

This works for 1–20 eggs

Joanna Trollope
AUTHORESS

Tuna and Cannellini Beans

4 tuna steaks
2 cans cannellini beans, drained and rinsed
2 red onions
2 cloves garlic
1 packet rocket leaves
Salt and pepper
2 lemons

1. Finely chop onions and garlic, put in saucepan with olive oil and sweat with lid on, over low heat for 5 minutes.
2. Add drained and rinsed beans then stir until mixed and hot.
3. Add salt and pepper. Turn off heat.
4. Stir torn rocket leaves into bean mixture until wilted.
5. Divide mixture between 4 plates.
6. Season tuna steaks, heat a very little oil and fry in hot griddle pan for 2–3 minutes each side.
7. Put a tuna steak on top of vegetables and squeeze over lemon juice.

Takes ten minutes!

SERVES 4

'There is no sight on earth more appealing than the sight of a woman making dinner for someone she loves.'
Thomas Wolfe

Rick Wakeman

MUSICIAN AND SONGWRITER

Henry VIII's Crunchy Pasta

I have no doubt that Henry VIII would have cooked this himself, had he had access to the ingredients, the necessary utensils and had spent less time in the bedroom and more time in the kitchen. So I've had to do it for him.

Having almost caught up with Henry VIII myself as regards the number of times I have said 'I do', there have been considerable periods of bachelor-hood in between these sorties into matrimony when I have needed to fend for myself in the kitchen and it was during one such episode in my life that the following recipe was born.

I will pre-warn anybody attempting the Henry VIII Pasta, that there may well be a few ingredients that do not tickle their personal taste buds and so quite simply, the rule is to leave those out, as there's certainly no shortage of other stuff to throw in the pan.

I also do not use conventional weights and measures, but I do think that everything will be perfectly understandable.

Select what you would like:
1 handful of minced steak, 2 handfuls if you have little hands
1 stick of celery, diced
1 handful of button mushrooms, sliced
4 large cloves of garlic, chopped
1 yellow pepper, chopped
1 leek, sliced
1 large Spanish onion, chopped
1 red onion, chopped
1 bunch of spring onions, sliced
2 large carrots, or a few smaller ones, diced
1 eggcup full of red wine vinegar
A dollop of brown sauce (Daddies or HP)
½ an eggcup of lemon juice
2 tablespoons of Worcestershire Sauce
1 tablespoon of soy sauce
Salt and pepper to taste
6 fresh basil leaves
2 tablespoons of dried Italian herbs
4 drips of Tabasco sauce
1 tin of chopped tomatoes
1 small jar of tomato pasta sauce, any type will do

Olive oil
1 large packet of pasta, any will do, but the shells work
    particularly well

You will need:
1 large wok, preferably with a lid
1 large saucepan
1 sieve

1. Chop or slice all the vegetables.
2. Heat the oil in the wok until it is very hot.
3. Add the garlic and mushrooms, stir, and when beginning to
brown add the onions, turning the heat down to half.
4. Now add the carrots, celery, leek, yellow pepper, spring onions,
stir well and then add the tin of chopped tomatoes.
5. Add all the other ingredients in any order you fancy and stir.
6. Reduce the heat to a simmer and cover with a lid.
7. Gently fry the mince until brown, drain off excess water and fat
and add to the wok.
8. Cook the pasta in boiling water for no more than 8 minutes.
9. Empty the pasta into a sieve and rinse with boiling water.
10. Sling the pasta into the wok and thoroughly mix in with the
'sauce'.
11. Turn up the heat a little and after five minutes of continual
stirring shout to everybody that it's ready.
12. Serve with freshly warmed crusty bread or garlic bread.
Open a bottle of whatever takes your fancy. You can drink anything
with this concoction!

This meal will happily serve either four hungry people or two fat
people.

'If the soup had been as warm as
the wine, if the wine had been as
old as the turkey, if the turkey had
had a breast like the maid, it would
have been a swell dinner.'
*Duncan Hines, American food
critic and writer of food and
lodging guidebooks*

The Duchess of Wellington MBE

Venison Steak Diane

4 x 6 oz steaks cut from a venison haunch, trimmed of fat
4 oz unsalted butter
Juice and rind of half a lemon
1 tablespoon chopped parsley
1 clove garlic
1 dessertspoon caster sugar
Worcestershire Sauce
½ tablespoon brandy – for flaming

1. Cut each steak in half and beat flat with a rolling pin until
½ inch thick. Place on a tray, separated by cling film.
2. Melt 2 oz butter in a large frying pan, crush the garlic into this.
When the butter foams, fry the steaks quickly, about 30 seconds
each side, then keep warm.
3. Melt the other 2 oz butter in a pan, add the lemon juice and
finely grated rind, the parsley, caster sugar and Worcestershire
Sauce to taste. Heat through, return the steaks to the pan and coat
in the sauce.
4. Add the brandy and set alight.

Serve with creamed potatoes and a suitable vegetable.

SERVES 4

Brian Wells

CHELSEA PENSIONER

In 1983 Brian Wells was in charge of catering for the rear party of the Queen's Own Highlanders while his regiment was in the Falklands. World Champion snooker player Steve Davis volunteered to play an exhibition match for the Garrison and this was the curry recipe that Brian cooked for him as a 'thank you'.

Lamb Vindaloo

2 tsp whole cumin seeds
2–3 hot, dried red chillies
1 tsp black peppercorns
1 tsp cardamom seeds
7.5cm/3 inch stick of cinnamon
1½ tsp black mustard seeds
1 tsp fenugreek seeds
5 tbsp white wine vinegar
Salt
Vegetable oil
1 tsp brown sugar
2 onions, sliced
4–6 tbsp water plus 225ml/8 fl oz
900g/2 lb boneless lamb cut into 2.5cm/1 inch cubes
5cm/2 inches fresh ginger, peeled and chopped
4 cloves of garlic
1 tbsp ground coriander seeds
½ tsp turmeric

1. Grind cumin seeds, chillies, peppercorns, cardamom seeds, cinnamon, black mustard seeds and fenugreek then add the vinegar, salt and sugar. Mix.
2. Heat the oil in a large pan and fry the onions, stirring, until brown and crisp.
Purée the onions in a blender with 2–3 tbsp water then add to the spices and vinegar. This vindaloo paste can be made in advance and frozen.
3. Blend the ginger and garlic with 2–3 tbsp water to make a paste.
4. Dry the meat then fry over high heat, a few pieces at a time, until brown on all sides. Remove meat from the pan.
5. Put the ginger and garlic paste into the pan, turn down the heat,

stir, then add coriander and turmeric.

6. Add the meat and juices, the vindaloo paste, 225ml/8 fl oz water and bring to the boil.

7. Cover and simmer gently for at least an hour until the lamb is tender, stirring occasionally.

8. Sprinkle with fresh coriander and serve with fluffy rice.

SERVES 6

Major General The Duke of Westminster
KG CB OBE TD DC DL

Roasted Woodcock with Quail Eggs on Potato Rosti

4 woodcock breasts
8 slices of smoked pancetta
4 quail eggs
2 large potatoes
Sprigs of fresh thyme
Olive oil

Pre heat oven to 200C/400F/Gas mark 6

1. Peel potatoes and boil them in lightly salted water for ten minutes, drain and leave to cool. Once cooled grate the potatoes and season with salt and pepper and add some thyme to flavour.
2. Taking the woodcock breasts wrap them with the smoked pancetta and again season with salt and pepper.
3. Heating up two oven-proof frying pans add a little olive oil to both pans. In one pan place all the woodcock breasts and brown gently on either side for 2 minutes each side and then place in the oven for 7 minutes.
4. In the other pan place your grated potato and form into round discs approx 3 inches in diameter and fry these until golden.
5. Take the potatoes and place them on a serving dish putting the roasted woodcock on top of the potato and top with a shallow fried quail egg.

SERVES 4

'Nothing would be more tiresome than eating and drinking if God had not made them a pleasure as well as a necessity.'
Voltaire

Antony Worral Thompson
CHEF AND RESTAURATEUR

Slow-Cooked Roast Pork Belly

1 teaspoon soft thyme leaves
1 tablespoon rosemary leaves, roughly chopped
2 tablespoons fresh sage leaves, roughly chopped
1 tablespoon fennel seeds
4 garlic cloves, finely chopped
2 tablespoons olive oil
15g/½ oz coarse salt
Coarsely ground black pepper
1 x 2kg/4½ pound piece of pork belly (ask the butcher to remove
    the ribs and trim off the excess fat)
3 tablespoons runny honey

1. Crush the herbs and garlic into a paste with the olive oil in a
mini food processor or mortar and pestle.
2. Lay the pork belly skin-side up. Score the skin in tight lines with
a Stanley Knife. Sprinkle the salt and coarsely ground black pepper
over it, rubbing them well into the meat with your fingers. Leave to
rest for 10 minutes so the salt and pepper settle well into the meat.
3. Rub the paste over the meat side, then leave to marinate
overnight.
4. Pre-heat the oven to its highest setting.
5. Place the pork on a bed of onions and carrots, skin side up and
roast it for 25 minutes. Then reduce the oven temperature to
150C/300F/Gas mark 2. Roast for two and half hours. If the
crackling gets too brown, loosely cover with the foil.
6. Remove the joint from the oven and coat with honey, drizzling
some of the juices from the roasting tin all over it too. Insert a fork
in either side of the joint and lift it on to a wooden board. If you
are serving the pork immediately, place the roasting tin on the hob
and stir with a wooden spoon, scraping up all the caramelised bits
from the base of the tin, until the juices from the meat reduce and
thicken slightly. Remove the crackling then slice the joint thinly and
serve with the juices and a chunk of crackling.

SERVES 10 –12

Antony Worral Thompson
CHEF AND RESTAURATEUR

Retro Chicken with Mushrooms and Bacon

The oldies are often great moreish dishes and this recipe combines many of the flavours that we all love.

4 free range chicken breasts
4 slices Parma ham
55g (2 oz) unsalted butter
115g (4 oz) smoked bacon lardons
1 onion, finely chopped
115g (4 oz) button mushrooms, halved
75ml (3 fl oz) chicken stock
75ml (3 fl oz) white wine
115g (4 oz) frozen petits pois
150ml (¼ pt) double cream
1 tsp plain flour

1. Wrap each chicken breast in a slice of Parma ham. If required secure with a cocktail stick.
2. Heat half the butter in a large frying pan and cook the chicken breasts for 3 minutes until the Parma ham is crispy all over. Remove from the frying pan to a flat roasting tray and pop in the oven at 180C/350F/Gas mark 4 for 12 minutes.
3. Meanwhile, add the bacon lardons to the chicken frying pan and cook until crisp – about 4 minutes, then add the onion and mushrooms and cook over a medium heat for 6 minutes until the onions have softened.
4. Pour the chicken stock into the frying pan and over a fierce heat reduce the liquid by half. Add the white wine and again reduce by half.
5. Add the peas and cook for 2 minutes, beat the cream with the flour and pour into the frying pan, cook for 5 minutes until thickened. Season to taste.
6. Remove the chicken from the oven to four warm plates, pour the sauce over and serve with new potatoes or mash.

SERVES 4

Aldo Zilli
CHEF

Spaghetti with Fresh Lobster

175g/6 oz spaghetti
Fresh basil sprigs to garnish

For the sauce:
900g/2 lb cooked lobsters
2 beef tomatoes, skinned and seeded
60ml/4 tbsp freshly chopped flat leaf parsley
60ml/4 tbsp freshly chopped basil
2 garlic cloves, peeled and finely chopped
Salt and freshly ground pepper
50ml/2 fl oz brandy
50ml/2 fl oz olive oil
1 small red onion, peeled and finely chopped
150ml/5 fl oz dry white wine

1. Split the lobster in half lengthways and break off the claws. Gently remove the lobster meat from the shells, trying to keep the claw meat intact. Chop the body meat. Wash the lobster body shells and set aside to use for presentation.
2. Chop the tomato flesh and place in a bowl with the parsley, basil and half of the garlic. Season with salt and freshly ground black pepper. Set aside.
3. In a large frying pan heat half of the oil and add the onion and remaining garlic. Stir in the lobster and pour over the brandy; ignite the alcohol to flambé. Once the flames have died down add the tomato mixture with the wine. Simmer for 5–8 minutes until the juices reduce slightly.
4. Meanwhile bring a large pan of salted water to the boil. Add the spaghetti and cook for 5–8 minutes or according to the instructions on the packet, until *al dente*. Drain and add to the lobster sauce, tossing well to mix. Adjust the seasoning if necessary.
5. If using the lobster shells for presentation place on 2 large serving plates or bowls and top with the spaghetti, spooning over the sauce. Drizzle over the remaining oil and garnish with basil sprigs and serve immediately.

SERVES 2

Field Marshals' Fare

Aunt Edith's Supper Dish
Roast Gammon with Rum, Raisin and Citrus Sauce
BBQ'd Grouse Stuffed with Haggis
Lamb Loin Stuffed with Figs, Fresh Herbs and Ginger
Fabulous Fish Stew
Cassoulet

Field Marshal the Lord Bramall
KG GCB OBE MC
CHIEF OF THE DEFENCE STAFF 1982–1985

Aunt Edith's Supper Dish

I would like to start my meal with chilled Beef Consommé, followed by Aunt Edith's Supper Dish and then Crêpes Suzettes for dessert.

Aunt Edith's Dish:
Sliced tomatoes
Fried onions
Hard boiled eggs with a little curry powder
1 pint cheese sauce
Cooked rice

1. In a greased oven-proof dish put a layer of sliced tomatoes. Season.
2. Fry the onions and put these on top, followed by some halved boiled eggs, sprinkled with a little curry powder.
3. Cover the eggs with the cheese sauce and top with a layer of cooked rice.
4. Cover the dish and heat in a moderate oven, 180C/350F/Gas mark 4 for about 25 minutes until hot right through.

Delicious!

'Bad men live that they may eat and drink, whereas good men eat and drink that they may live'
Socrates

154

Field Marshal Sir John Chapple
GCB CBE DL
CHIEF OF THE DEFENCE STAFF 1989–1992

Roast Gammon with Rum, Raisin and Citrus Sauce

Prime gammon joint
Black treacle
Salt crystals

Sauce:
1 orange
1 lime
3 oz raisins
4 oz dark brown sugar
Arrowroot

Make sauce the day beforehand:

1. Zest orange and lime and slice outer skin into very thin strips.
Squeeze juice from both.
2. Place all in a saucepan with the raisins and the sugar. Whisk
arrowroot into the mix.
3. Put saucepan on low heat, whisking until simmering. When
sauce turns clear, remove from heat, cool and then chill.
4. Dry skin of gammon and make cuts, scoring across the whole
skin. Let skin dry by using kitchen paper or leave standing in
refrigerator.
5. When ready to cook turn oven to 240C/475F/Gas mark 9.
6. Lightly coat gammon with warm treacle and sprinkle with salt
crystals. Put in roasting tin, skin side up and put in oven.
7. After 25 minutes turn oven down to 180C/350F/Gas mark 4
8. Cook for 2 hours then take out of oven, cover with foil and let
the gammon rest.
9. Serve with crackling and the sauce poured over.

155

Field Marshal
HRH The Duke of Edinburgh

KG KT OM GBE PC

WINDSOR CASTLE

BBQ'd Grouse Stuffed with Haggis

Grouse (1 per person)
Herb paste
Haggis
Pin-head oatmeal

1. Mash the haggis with a little oatmeal to make it slightly less 'gooey'.
2. Clean the grouse and remove the legs – there is not much on them anyway and they tend to get in the way while cooking on the grill.
3. Stuff the stuffing into the cavity.
4. Cover the breasts of the grouse liberally with the herb paste. The composition of the herb paste is a matter of personal choice.
5. Cook the grouse on its back for 20 minutes over a medium heat. It doesn't matter whether the back gets a bit burnt as it won't be eaten, but it does not want to be incinerated.
6. Turn the bird over on to one side and cook the breasts for between 3 and 7 minutes each, depending on how 'well-done' you wish the flesh to be. After 3 minutes on each side it should be 'rare' and after about 7 minutes on each side it should be cooked through.

Field Marshal the Lord Inge KG GCB DL

CHIEF OF THE DEFENCE STAFF 1994–1997

Lamb Loin Stuffed with Figs, Fresh Herbs and Ginger

600g boneless eye of lamb loin
8 slices of rindless streaky bacon
4–5 dried figs, roughly chopped
8 leaves of fresh mint and basil
2 shallots and 1 clove garlic, finely chopped
1 tsp of fresh ginger, peeled and minced
2 tbsp virgin olive oil
3 slices of white bread
1 tsp of lemon juice
1 egg yolk
Rock salt and freshly ground black pepper

Pancakes:
60g plain flour plus a pinch of salt
1 egg
1 tbsp vegetable oil
100ml milk plus 50ml water mixed together

1. Sieve the flour and salt into a bowl, make a well in the centre and crack in the egg. Beat the egg into the flour then gradually stir in the liquid until smooth. Stir in the oil and stand for 30 minutes before using.
2. Heat a frying pan and make 2 thin pancakes.
3. In a pan heat the oil, add shallot, garlic and ginger and cook until translucent. Add the figs, stir and cook for 2 minutes. Liquidise in a food processor then add the bread, lemon juice, mint, basil and egg yolk to make a rough stuffing.
4. Butterfly and flatten out the lamb then season with salt and pepper. Put the stuffing in the middle of the lamb and roll up. Wrap and seal the loin in pancakes. Pull the streaky bacon with a knife to make it thin, wrap it round the lamb, brush with oil then place on an oiled tray.
5. Roast at 200C/400F/Gas mark 6 for about 30 minutes. Take out and rest for 10 minutes then cut in 20mm slices and serve with redcurrant jus.

SERVES 4

157

Field Marshal HRH The Duke of Kent
KG GCMG GCVO

THE OFFICE OF HRH THE DUKE OF KENT
ST. JAMES'S PALACE
LONDON SW1A 1BQ

Fabulous Fish Stew

2 cloves of garlic, peeled

250ml ready-made mayonnaise

Lemon juice

12 mussels

20 clams

A small wineglass of white wine

400g good-quality tinned plum tomatoes

2 small fillets of seabass or bream, cut in half

2 small fillets of red mullet or snapper, cut in half

2 small fillets of monkfish or other firm white fish

4 langoustines or tiger prawns, shell on

2 thick slices of crusty bread

A small handful of fennel tops

A small bunch of fresh basil, leaves picked and stalks chopped

Extra virgin olive oil

Sea salt and freshly ground black pepper

A small pinch of saffron, optional

1. To make the saffron aioli, smash a clove of garlic, a tiny squeeze of lemon juice and the saffron (if using) with a small pinch of salt in a pestle and mortar until it turns into a mush. Add a tablespoon of mayonnaise and pound again. Stir in the rest of the mayo. Taste and season with a little more lemon juice, salt and pepper.

2. Give the mussels and clams a good wash in plenty of clean, cold water and scrub any dirty ones lightly with a scrubbing brush, pulling off any beardy bits. If there are any that aren't tightly closed, give them a sharp tap. If they don't close up, throw them away.

3. Heat a large, wide saucepan or stewing pot and pour in a splash of olive oil. Slice up the other clove of garlic and fry it in the oil until lightly golden. Add the wine and the tomatoes and the basil stalks and bring to the boil. Simmer gently for 10 to 15 minutes until the liquid has reduced a little.

4. Add all your fish and shellfish in a single layer and season with salt and pepper. Push the fish down into the liquid and put the lid on. Cook gently for about 10 minutes or until all the clams and mussels have opened and the fish fillets and langoustines or prawns are cooked through. (Discard any clams or mussels that don't open.)

5. Toast the bread on a hot griddle pan and get out the serving bowls. Put a piece of toast in each bowl and ladle the soup over the top, making sure the fish is divided more or less evenly. Top each bowl with some fennel tops, basil leaves, a drizzle of extra virgin olive oil and a big blob of saffron aioli.

SERVES 2

Field Marshal the Lord Vincent
GBE KCB DSO
CHIEF OF THE DEFENCE STAFF 1991-1993, CHAIR OF THE MILITARY COMMITTEE OF NATO 1993-1996

Cassoulet

2½–3 lb chicken
1 lb haricot beans, soaked overnight
1 lb onions, peeled
4 whole cloves
1 bay leaf
½ lb piece bacon, rinded and diced
Parsley stalks
2 oz butter
2 cloves garlic, peeled and crushed
½ lb garlic sausage, skinned and sliced
1 level teaspoon dried thyme
½ pint milk
Salt and pepper

1. Put the drained, soaked and rinsed beans in a large pan, cover with salted water. Add one small onion studded with cloves, bay leaf, bacon rind and parsley stalks.
2. Simmer, covered, until the beans are tender but not broken up, about 1¾ hours. The water should have been absorbed.
3. Roast the chicken for about ¾ hour at 200C/400F/Gas mark 6. Divide into 8 portions.
4. Fry the remaining sliced onions in butter until golden brown. Add garlic.
5. Lightly stir the bacon, sausage, fried onions and thyme into the beans. Adjust seasoning and turn into a large casserole.
6. Push the chicken portions into the beans and pour over ½ pint hot milk. Cover tightly with a lid. Cook in oven at 160C/325F/Gas mark 3 for about 1 hour.
7. Serve with tomato and watercress salad.

SERVES 8

Desserts

Chocolate Trifle
Brown Bread Ice Cream
Creamed Rice Pudding
Brown Bread Ice Cream with Raspberries
Rhubarb and Jelly Mousse
Doppio Cioccolato con Pistachio – Double Chocolate Mousse with Pistachio Nuts
Bread and Butter Pudding
Mary Berry's Basic Special Ice Cream
White Chocolate, Whisky and Croissant Butter Pudding
Cheat's Ten-minute Strawberry Gateau
Vanilla Almond Shortbread
Bread and Butter Pudding
Mulled Autumn Fruit
Lizzie's Orange and Almond Pudding
Hampshire Roll
Baked Egg Custard with Garibaldi Biscuits
Cider Baked Apples with a Maize Crust
Wineberries with Coconut Cookies

Jane Asher
ACTRESS AND CAKE MAKER

Chocolate Trifle

This luxurious version of an old favourite is easy to do and makes a delicious change from the usual recipe. It's easy to vary the ingredients too: you could use rum or whisky instead of the brandy for example (or orange juice if you want to keep it alcohol-free), and ready to eat apricots or plums instead of the prunes. You may need to walk a few extra times round the beautiful Royal Hospital grounds if you eat a large portion . . .

275g (9 oz) dark chocolate
3 chocolate muffins
125g (4 oz) ready to eat prunes
1 tablespoon (60ml) brandy
2 large oranges, peeled, pithed and segmented
1 pint (600ml) ready-made custard
100g (3½ oz) Amaretti biscuits
284ml (10 fl oz) double cream, lightly whipped

1. Start by melting the chocolate in a bowl over simmering water or in the microwave.
2. Slice the muffins and place in the bottom of a trifle dish and drizzle the brandy over them. Add the prunes.
3. Segment the oranges and layer over the prunes, then spoon the fresh custard over the oranges. Scatter the Amaretti biscuits over the custard.
4. Take the chocolate off the heat, let it cool slightly then stir into the lightly whipped cream.
5. Spoon the chocolate and cream mixture over the trifle and decorate with chocolate curls or shavings. Chill well in the fridge before serving.

Calories per portion: 750

SERVES 6–8

'A prune is an experienced plum.'
John Trattner, US writer and journalist

Carole Bamford
DAYLESFORD ORGANIC

Brown Bread Ice Cream

45g/1½ oz wholemeal breadcrumbs
500ml/16 fl oz whipping cream
180g/6½ oz Demerara sugar
3 tablespoons dark rum
½ tsp vanilla extract

1. Spread out the breadcrumbs evenly on a baking tray and toast under the grill, turning them so they brown evenly.
2. Measure the whipping cream into a jug and stir in the cooled brown crumbs, with the sugar, rum and vanilla extract.
3. Cover and chill for an hour to give the crumbs a chance to soften then churn in an ice-cream machine according to manufacturer's instructions.
Serve as fresh as possible.

'**Bread deals with living things, with giving life, with growth, with the seed, the grain that nurtures. It is not coincidence that we say bread is the staff of life.**' *Lionel Poilane, French Master Baker*

Joe Britton

CHELSEA PENSIONER

Creamed Rice Pudding

Mr Britton, aged 98, is our oldest In-Pensioner and in April 2009 he appeared on Channel 4's *Deal or No Deal* and won £20,000. Not only did he most generously give half to the Royal Hospital but he wowed the audience and received the first standing ovation on the programme. Mr Britton cooked at home when he could and rice pudding is his favourite recipe:

190g/6½ oz pudding rice
2.1 litres/3½ pints milk
1 beaten egg
75g/3 oz sugar
Nutmeg to taste

1. Wash and pick over the rice. Bring the milk to the boil, sprinkle in the rice and sugar and re-boil, stirring all the time.
2. Simmer for 10 minutes then add 1 beaten egg.
3. Put in well-buttered baking dish and sprinkle with nutmeg.
4. Place in oven 150C/300F/ Gas mark 2 for 1 hour or until rice grains are tender.

SERVES 2

Photograph © Endemol

The Duchess of Buccleuch & Queensbury
Brown Bread Ice Cream with Raspberries

This is an all time family favourite, based on a Victorian recipe, and first used as far as I can tell, in the kitchen at Drumlanrig Castle in Dumfriesshire. It is easy to make, and delicious to eat at any time of the year.

600ml whole milk
227ml double cream
4 large egg yolks
175g golden granulated sugar
75g wholemeal bread, crusts cut off
125g raspberries, to serve.

1. Gently heat the milk and cream in a small pan until steaming. In a mixing bowl, whisk together the yolks and 50g of the sugar until thick, then pour on the milk. Wash out the pan, return the mixture to it and cook gently for 6–7 minutes until it lightly coats the back of the spoon. Cool, and then place in the fridge while you make the caramel crumbs.
2. Preheat the grill to high. Whizz the bread into crumbs in a food processor and mix these with the remaining 125g sugar. Spread on a baking sheet, place 10cm from the grill and watch, regularly re-spreading the crumbs until the mixture is a dark gold. This will take about 10–12 minutes.
3. Remove and cool. Break into large pieces (a rolling pin may be required if your caramel is very hard). Stir into the custard mix.
If using an ice-cream maker, return to the fridge for 20 minutes to allow the caramel to release its flavour. Churn for 20 minutes.
If you don't own an ice-cream maker, place in a plastic container in the freezer for 2 hours; take out, whisk and freeze for an hour, repeat the whisking then freeze until ready. Allow to soften for 25 minutes before serving with raspberries.

SERVES 4

The Earl and Countess Cadogan
GREAT FRIENDS AND SUPPORTERS OF THE ROYAL HOSPITAL

Rhubarb and Jelly Mousse

8 sticks rhubarb
10 tbsp sugar
2 tbsp crème fraiche
2 tbsp Greek yoghurt
2 egg whites
Gelatine
Hot water

1. Cut rhubarb into 2 inch chunks. Place in a large ovenproof dish, sprinkle sugar over fruit then sprinkle a little water over to wet the sugar. Cover with foil and bake at 160C/325F/Gas mark 3 for about 25 minutes until tender. Remove dish from the oven once during cooking and baste liquid over fruit.
2. Place large sieve over bowl and pour fruit into sieve. Drain all liquid from rhubarb. Measure the bright pink syrup then put to one side.
3. Mash or purée sieved rhubarb and then put into a bowl. Add more sugar if needed and leave to cool completely.
4. Mix crème fraiche and yoghurt into rhubarb and then lightly fold in stiffly whipped egg whites.
5. Spoon into 6 pretty stemmed glasses or suitable bowls until about ½ full. Put in the fridge to chill for about an hour.
1 sachet of gelatine will set 1 pint of liquid. Measure gelatine, according to amount of liquid reserved, and sprinkle it onto 4 fl oz hot water, mix well to dissolve, then add pink liquid, stir and let it cool.
6. Remove mousse from fridge, gently spoon about ½ inch jelly on top of mousse then return to fridge to set for several hours.
Place on small plates and serve.

SERVES 6

Gino D'Acampo
CHEF

Doppio Cioccolato con Pistachio
Double Chocolate Mousse with Pistachio Nuts

150g dark chocolate (good quality and chopped)
100g white chocolate (good quality and chopped)
3 fresh eggs
2 tbsp caster sugar
2 tbsp Amaretto liquor
250ml softly whipped cream
2 handfuls of crushed pistachio nuts

1. Melt the chocolate in a glass bowl over a pan with hot water (don't let the bowl touch the water). Once melted, set aside to cool, but not to harden.
2. Beat the eggs and sugar in a bowl until thick and pale. With the help of a metal spoon fold the chocolate into the egg mixture. Add in the nuts and Amaretto liquor, mix well and then gently fold in the whipped cream.
3. Place the mixture into four separate dessert glasses (approx. 250ml), refrigerate for 3 hours until set. Just before serving decorate with some crushed pistachio nuts on top.

SERVES 4

'Just give me chocolate and
nobody gets hurt.'

Dame Judi Dench CH DBE FRSA

ACTRESS

Bread and Butter Pudding

This is delicious and provides the perfect solution for what to do with those dry Italian cakes you get given at Christmas!

> 275ml/½ pint of milk
> 70ml/⅛ pint double cream
> Grated rind of half a small lemon
> 50g/2 oz castor sugar
> 3 eggs
> Pannetone cake
> 10g/½ oz candied lemon or orange peel, finely chopped
> 50g/2 oz currants
> Freshly grated nutmeg

> Heat oven to 180C/350F/Gas mark 4

1. Butter a 2 pint (1 litre) oblong enamel baking dish.
2. Slice the Pannetone and butter it. Put one layer on the base of the dish, sprinkle with the candid peel and half the currants.
3. Put another layer of Pannetone in the dish and sprinkle with the rest of the currants.
4. Put the milk and cream together in a measuring jug, stir in the lemon peel and sugar. Whisk the eggs in a small basin and add to the milk mixture.
5. Pour the whole lot over the Pannetone and sprinkle with freshly grated nutmeg.
6. Bake in the oven for 30–40 minutes. Serve warm.

'Oh, a wonderful pudding!'
Bob Cratchit said, and calmly
too, that he regarded it as
the greatest success achieved
by Mrs Cratchit since their
marriage.
Charles Dickens

171

Sue MacGregor CBE

RADIO PRESENTER

Mary Berry's Basic Special Ice Cream

Many years ago, when I presented *Woman's Hour* on Radio 4, I was lucky enough to watch famous cooks do their stuff in the studio and collect the recipes afterwards.

One of the cooks was the wonderful Mary Berry, whose simple and delicious basic ice cream recipe does not need to be taken out of the freezer and re-whisked, which is good news in my book.

You can add your own favourite fruit purée just before freezing – mine is strawberry.

4 eggs, separated
100g (4 oz) caster sugar
300ml (½ pint) double cream

1. Whisk the yolks in a small bowl.
2. Whisk the egg whites in a larger bowl until stiff, then whisk in the sugar a teaspoonful at a time. The whites will get stiffer with each spoonful.
3. Whisk the cream until it forms soft peaks and fold it into the meringue mixture with the egg yolks.
4. Stir in 150ml (¼ pint) fruit purée just before freezing.

Raspberry or gooseberry purée are of course as delicious as strawberry. Turn into a 1.4 litre container, cover, label and freeze.

SERVES 6–8

James Martin
Chef

White Chocolate, Whisky and Croissant Butter Pudding

500ml milk
500ml double cream
1 vanilla pod
3 whole eggs
5 egg yolks
200g caster sugar
4 large croissants
25g sultanas
25g butter, melted
175g white chocolate, grated
3 tbsp whisky
55g apricot jam
Icing Sugar
Vanilla ice cream

1. Pre-heat the oven to 200C/400F/Gas mark 6. Pour the milk and cream into a pan, add the vanilla pod, and gradually bring to the boil.
2. Place the eggs, egg yolks and sugar together in the mixing bowl with the whisk attachment and mix gently on a low setting.
3. While the cream is heating, slice the croissants and place in an ovenproof dish, slightly overlapping the pieces. Sprinkle with sultanas and pour over the butter.
4. Once the cream has boiled, take it off the heat. Add the egg mixture and chocolate and stir well. Set on one side to allow the chocolate to melt, stirring occasionally.
5. Add the whisky to the cream mixture. Next, using a sieve, strain the cream over the croissants, cover with foil and bake in the oven for 15-20 minutes or until almost set.
6. Remove from the oven, coat the top with the jam, and dust with icing sugar. Caramelize the topping using a very hot grill or, if you have one, a blow-torch. This is best served at room temperature, with a spoonful of good quality ice cream.

SERVES 4

Nick Nairn
CHEF AND RESTAURATEUR

Cheat's Ten-minute Strawberry Gateau

1 x 250g (9 oz) sponge flan case
600ml (1 pint) double cream
25g (1 oz) caster sugar
2 tablespoons (approx) brandy
1½ x 250g (9 oz) punnets strawberries
55g (2 oz) icing sugar
Few sprigs fresh mint
Spun-sugar topping 175g (6 oz) caster sugar

1. Cut out the centre of the flan, using a 20-25 cm (8–10 in) stainless-steel ring (or the ring of a spring-form cake tin, without the base). With a sharp knife, carefully cut this sponge disc in half through the middle so you end up with two thin discs. Place the ring on a surface or tray, and put one of the discs inside it.
2. Whip the double cream with the sugar and brandy until thick. Keep in the fridge.
3. Hull the strawberries. Leave some whole for a garnish (about ten of the small ones), and cut the rest in half lengthways. Line the ring with the largest strawberry halves, cut side against the ring. You won't need all of them at this stage.
4. Spoon the chilled, whipped cream into the ring and gently press to the edges, keeping the strawberries in place against the sides. Arrange the rest of the halved strawberries over the top. Add the other sponge disc, and press it down. Dust generously with icing sugar. Lift the cake on to a plate. Remove the ring by carefully warming the edges with a hot cloth and lifting it straight off.
5. Place the sugar for the spun sugar into a very clean pan and heat. Once caramelized – golden brown and sizzling – remove from the heat to cool slightly.
6. While this is cooling, take a metal skewer and hold it in a gas flame until it is red hot. Use it to score the top of the gateau in lines to create a diamond pattern. Decorate the top with the left-over strawberries and berries, and garnish with sprigs of fresh mint.
7. To finish, dip a small spoon into the caramelized sugar and twist it around a steel to create some sugar curls. Continue doing this until you have a candyfloss texture. Place this on top of the berries and serve.

Gordon Ramsay
CHEF AND RESTAURATEUR

Vanilla Almond Shortbread

My kids absolutely love shortbread and these don't last very long in my house. The almonds give the shortbread a different crunch and a slightly nutty flavour that complements the vanilla.

200g plain flour
¼ tsp fine sea salt
225g unsalted butter, softened
125g golden caster sugar, plus extra to sprinkle
1 vanilla pod
150g ground almonds

1. Sift the flour with the salt. Put the butter and sugar into a mixing bowl. Slice the vanilla pod open and scrape out the seeds with the back of the knife. Add the seeds to the butter and sugar and beat with an electric mixer until smooth and creamy.
2. Using a wooden spoon, stir in the flour and salt followed by the ground almonds. Press the mixture into a dough, wrap with cling film and chill for at least 30 minutes.
3. Preheat the oven to 180C/350F/Gas mark 4. Roll out the dough on a lightly floured board, about 5–7mm thick. Slice into finger lengths or cut out rounds using a pastry cutter, then transfer to 2 lightly greased baking sheets. Remember to leave a little space between each biscuit. Prick each biscuit lightly with a fork.
4. Bake for about 15–20 minutes until pale golden. As soon as it comes out of the oven, sprinkle with a little golden caster sugar. Let the shortbread cool on the tray for 10 minutes until firm, then transfer to a wire rack to cool completely.

Keep in an airtight container and enjoy within a week or two.

MAKES ABOUT 20–25

Gary Rhodes
CHEF AND RESTAURATEUR

Bread and Butter Pudding

12 medium slices white bread, crusts cut off
50g unsalted butter, softened
1 vanilla pod or few drops of vanilla essence
400ml double cream
400ml milk
8 egg yolks
175g caster sugar, plus extra for the caramelised topping
25g sultanas
25g raisins

1. Split the vanilla pod and place in a saucepan with the cream and milk and bring to the boil. While it is heating, whisk together the egg yolks and caster sugar in a bowl. Allow the cream mix to cool a little then strain it on to the egg yolks, stirring all the time. You now have the custard.
2. Butter the bread, cut it into triangular quarters or halves and arrange in the buttered 1.5–1.8 litre dish in three layers, sprinkling the fruit between two layers and leaving the top clear.
3. Now pour over the warm custard, lightly pressing the bread to help it soak in, and leave it to stand for at least 20–30 minutes before cooking to ensure that the bread absorbs all the custard.

The pudding can be prepared to this stage several hours in advance and cooked when needed.

5. Place the dish in a roasting tray three-quarters filled with warm water and bake at 180C/350F/Gas mark 4 for 20–30 minutes until the pudding begins to set. Don't overcook it or the custard will scramble.
6. Remove the pudding from the water bath, sprinkle it liberally with caster sugar and glaze under the grill on a medium heat or with a gas gun to a crunchy golden finish. When glazing, the sugar dissolves and caramelises, and you may find that the corners of the bread begin to burn. This helps the flavour, giving a bittersweet taste that mellows when it is eaten with the rich custard, which seeps out of the wonderful bread sponge when you cut into it.

Serves 6–8

Philippe Saint Romas
EXECUTIVE CHEF – RÉMY MARTIN

A Duo of Coeur de Cognac Desserts
This tempting duo of sweet treats was created by Philippe Saint Romas, the Executive Chef of the renowned cognac house of Rémy Martin, in celebration of the launch of their new cognac, Coeur de Cognac.
Distilled to a unique recipe, Coeur de Cognac is unlike any other and with its distinctive fruit-forward character and unrivalled smooth finish it is particularly suited to sweet morsels and delicious desserts. Enjoy!

White Chocolate, Apricot and Pistachio Cookie

680g unsalted butter
840g sugar
20g salt
7 whole eggs
1.1kg plain white flour
550g pecan nuts
800g white chocolate
200g pistachios
150g diced dried apricots

1. Mix the butter with the salt, add the sugar, flour, then the eggs and finally the remaining ingredients.
2. Form into balls (10g approx.) and arrange them in staggered rows on a baking tray covered with grease proof paper. Cover everything with cling film and then apply pressure in order to form cookie shapes.
3. Remove the cling film and bake at 200C/400F/Gas mark 6 to a very light golden colour. Remove from the baking tray and allow to cool on a rack.

Raspberry and Lavender Fruit Jellies

500g raspberry purée
60g caster sugar
12g yellow pectin
100g apple juice
550g granulated sugar
120g glucose
15g lemon juice
10g raspberry liqueur (crème de framboise)
10 drops of lavender extract

1. Bring the raspberry purée and apple juice to the boil. Remove from the heat and slowly sprinkle in half of the sugar and the yellow pectin, whilst whisking all the time. Return to the heat and cook at 107°C for 3 minutes, adding the remaining sugar and the glucose.
2. Remove from the heat and add the lemon juice, raspberry liqueur and lavender extract and leave to cool. Strain through a coulis purée sieve and spoon into silicone moulds (small hemispheres) and allow to set.
3. Once set, turn out of the moulds and roll in granulated sugar. To store, cover with parchment and keep in a cool, dry environment (avoid humidity).

Quinlan Terry
ARCHITECT

Mulled Autumn Fruit

2 eating apples
2 ripe pears (Conference are best)
4 dark red plums
½ bottle of red wine
3 tbsp Demerara sugar
Spices: cinnamon, cloves, nutmeg or ready-made mulled wine can be used but omit spices and reduce sugar to 2 tbsp

1. Peel, core and quarter apples and pears.
2. Halve and stone plums.
3. Cover the apples and pears with wine.
4. Add sugar and spices and simmer for 25-30 minutes or until the pears are tender.
5. Add plums for the last 15 minutes of cooking.
6. Serve hot or cold with ginger ice cream or crème fraiche.

SERVES 4–6

Lizzie's Orange and Almond Pudding

4 oranges
4 eggs separated
4 oz caster sugar
4 oz ground almonds

1. Grease and line a 7 inch round sandwich tin.
2. Zest and squeeze the oranges.
3. Beat egg yolks and sugar until light and creamy.
4. Fold in beaten egg whites, sugar, almonds and orange zest.
5. Cook in moderate oven 180C/350F/Gas mark 4 for about 20 minutes.
6. Turn out into a shallow bowl and soak with orange juice, which should stand around the cake. If there is not enough juice, squeeze more oranges!

SERVES 8

Brian Turner CBE
CHEF

Hampshire Roll

8 oz unsalted butter
6 oz caster sugar
3 medium eggs
2 tbsp double cream
Finely grated zest of 1 orange
6 oz plain sifted flour
A pinch salt
1½ lb apples (Cox or Granny Smith)
6 oz apricot jam
Icing sugar

Preheat the oven to 180C/350F/Gas mark 4.
Use 2 oz of the butter to generously grease a semi circular tray mould if you can find one or a large pie dish or 12 individual moulds.

1. To make the sponge, cream the sugar and remaining butter together until light then beat in the eggs, double cream and orange zest.
2. Fold in the flour and salt.
3. Peel, core and slice the apples, spread 4 oz of jam in the bottom of the mould or dish. Sprinkle over half the apples then spoon in half the sponge mixture.
4. Mix the remaining apple and jam together, place on top of the sponge in the mould then cover with the rest of the sponge.
5. Smooth the top and bake in the oven for 40-50 minutes until golden.
6. Serve sprinkled with icing sugar and accompanied by something like a vanilla clotted cream or hot custard.

SERVES 12

Marcus Wareing
CHEF AND RESTAURATEUR

Baked Egg Custard
with Garibaldi Biscuits

This is an old family favourite first made by my Nan. I made it for The Queen's 80th Birthday Celebration at Mansion House as part of the BBC *Great British Menu* series: I believe it is a truly British dessert. It is so popular we still serve it in the restaurant as guests complain if I remove it from the menu!

For the Garibaldi biscuits:
100g/3½ oz butter, melted in a saucepan
100g/3½ oz icing sugar, sifted
100g/3½ oz plain flour, plus extra for dusting
100g/3½ oz egg whites
200g/7 oz currants

For the pastry:
225g/8 oz flour, plus extra for dusting
pinch of salt
1 lemon, zest only
150g/5½ oz butter
75g/3 oz caster sugar
1 free-range egg yolk
1 free-range egg

For the custard filling:
9 free-range egg yolks
75g/3 oz caster sugar
500ml/17 fl oz whipping cream
freshly grated nutmeg

1. Preheat the oven to 180C/350F/Gas mark 4.
2. First, make the biscuits. Mix together the butter, icing sugar and flour until smooth. Slowly add the egg whites, stirring, until they are completely incorporated, then fold in the currants. Bring together into a ball, wrap in cling film and chill for at least one hour.
3. Roll out the dough on a lightly floured surface to 5mm/⅕in thick. Cut into 12 rectangles - you may have some dough left over. Place on a baking tray lined with greaseproof paper, ensuring the biscuits

are not touching each other. Chill in the fridge for 30 minutes.

4. Bake the biscuits for 8–10 minutes or until golden brown. Remove and cool on a wire rack. Keep in an airtight tin.

5. For the pastry, rub together the flour, salt, lemon zest and butter until the mixture resembles breadcrumbs. Add the sugar, then beat together the egg yolk and whole egg and slowly add these, mixing until the pastry forms a ball. Wrap tightly in cling film and refrigerate for two hours.

6. Turn the oven down to 170C/325F/Gas mark 3.

7. Roll out the pastry on a lightly floured surface to 2mm/⅛ inch thickness. Use to line an 18cm/7 in flan ring placed on a baking sheet. Line with greaseproof paper and fill with baking beans, then bake blind for about 10 minutes or until the pastry is starting to turn golden brown. Remove the paper and beans, and allow to cool.

8. Turn the oven down to 130C/250F/Gas mark 1.

9. For the filling, whisk together the yolks and sugar. Add the cream and mix well. Pass the mixture through a fine sieve into a saucepan and heat through. Do not boil.

10. Fill the pastry case with the custard, until 5mm/½ in from the top. Carefully place in the middle of the oven and bake for 30–40 minutes or until the custard appears set but not too firm. Remove from the oven and cover the surface liberally with grated nutmeg. Allow to cool to room temperature.

11. Before serving, warm the biscuits through in the oven for 5 minutes. Cut the tart with a sharp knife and serve with the biscuits.

The Garibaldi biscuit, currants squashed between two thin, oblong biscuits, was named after Giuseppe Garibaldi (1807–1882), the Italian general and leader of the fight to unify Italy. It was first manufactured in Bermondsey by Peek Freans in 1861

Lesley Waters
CHEF

Cider Baked Apples with a Maize Crust

Serve this mulled pie with thick Dorset cream or vanilla ice-cream

For the pastry:
140g (6 oz) plain flour
55g (2 oz) instant dried polenta or semolina
Pinch salt
115g (4 oz) butter
1 large egg, beaten
Cold water

For the filling:
6 large dessert apples, peeled, cored and halved
55g (2 oz) unsalted butter, melted
150ml (¼ pint) fruity cider
25g (1 oz) soft brown sugar
Sprig rosemary
Caster sugar for sprinkling

Preheat the oven to 200C/400F/Gas mark 6
1. Into a large bowl, sieve the flour, salt and polenta. Rub in the butter until the mixture resembles fine breadcrumbs. Stir in the egg and enough water to bind the dough together. Chill the pastry for 30 minutes.
2. Place the apples in a shallow, round oven proof dish approx. 23cm in diameter. Combine the melted butter with the cider and pour over the apples. Sprinkle the apples with the brown sugar and tuck in the sprig of rosemary.
3. On a lightly floured surface, roll out the pastry until it is large enough to lie as a blanket over the apples. Carefully lift the pastry over the apples and roughly trim the edges and tuck inside the dish.
4. Lightly sprinkle the pastry with the caster sugar.
5. Bake the pie for 10 minutes, then reduce the oven to 180C/350F/Gas Mark 4. Bake for a further 30-35 minutes until the apples are softened and cooked.

SERVES 6–8

The Duchess of Wellington MBE
Wineberries with Coconut Cookies

We have grown wineberries successfully for many years. They are originally from Japan and are especially good as they come into season as the raspberries are finishing.

2 egg whites
175g caster sugar
175g desiccated coconut

1. Whisk the egg whites just to a foam.
2. Add sugar and coconut.
3. Drop small spoonfuls onto a greased baking tray.
4. Bake in oven at 180C/350F/Gas mark 4 for 15 minutes.

Serve with berries and cream.

SERVES 4

'Tell me what you eat, and I
will tell you what you are.
Savarin

Baking

Chocolate Cake
Everyday Bread
Chocolate Fudge Cake
Honey Buns
Malt Loaf
My Nan's Lemon Drizzle Cake
Welsh Cakes
Chocolate Buns
Chunky Orange Marmalade
Snow-flecked Brownies
Sephardic Orange Cake
Dark Chocolate and Ginger Squares
Banana Bread
Roux's Chelsea Buns
Parkin

. . . And finally
Leather Bottle Wine

Cherie Blair
Chocolate Cake

100g (4 oz) soft margarine
100g (4 oz) cocoa powder
300g soft brown sugar
2 eggs
250ml milk
200g self-raising flour
1 tsp baking powder

Fudge Topping:
200g plain chocolate
175ml double cream
25g butter, diced

Pre-heat the oven to 180C/350F/Gas mark 4.
1. Cream together the margarine and sugar until light and fluffy.
2. Beat the eggs and mix with the cocoa powder.
3. Gradually add the egg and cocoa powder to the creamed margarine and sugar.
4. Sift together the flour and baking powder and fold this into the first mixture, then gradually mix in the milk until well blended.
5. Line and grease two 8" (20cm) sandwich tins and spoon the mixture into each of the tins.
6. Bake for about 30 minutes until risen and slightly firm to the touch. Allow to cool down a little, then remove from the tins and place the cakes on a wire cooling rack.
To prepare the fudge topping:
7. Heat the cream in a saucepan until boiling. Remove from the heat and stir in the chocolate, broken into pieces, until melted.
8. Finally beat in the butter and allow to cool down a little before using this to sandwich the cakes together and cover the top and sides of the cake.
Suitable for freezing without the icing and decoration

MAKES 8 PORTIONS

Emma Bridgewater
CERAMIC DESIGNER

Everyday Bread

One of my very favourite things to make is bread. This recipe is dead easy. It's exactly what my Mum always did, though she sometimes did it with 'real' yeast, which I seldom manage.

MAKES 3 LOAVES:

1. Take a large bowl – I use one from an old ewer and basin set, about 2 feet across and fairly shallow, but any large mixing bowl will do. Pour in 3lb organic whole meal stone-ground flour or any strong flour. My children much prefer white – they usually get a mixture.

2. Sprinkle in 3 teaspoonfuls of sea salt, and the same quantity of brown sugar.

3. Mix and add ONE sachet of quick acting yeast (the instructions on the yeast packet will urge you to use 2 sachets, but trust me one will do!)

4. Pour in about 1½ pint warm (blood heat) water.

5. Now mix using only your right hand, well floured, (assuming you are right-handed), try to keep your left hand more or less dough-free as the telephone is bound to ring in the next 5 minutes! The dough will come together slowly – put some more flour onto your kneading hand then you can start to knead, pulling the far side of the dough towards you and folding it over on itself whilst turning the bowl with your other hand. Add a sprinkle of flour if it is too sticky to work or a splash of water if it's too dry. Keep kneading for a few minutes until the consistency becomes elastic. If this sounds too much like work simply up the water to 2 pints and stir it into the flour using a large wooden spoon.

6. Tear into 3 equal size lumps, put (or pour the wetter version) into 3 greased 2 pint tins.

7. Leave in a draught-free place covered with a clean tea towel (please, no cling film, what is all that about?) until it has doubled in size. I sometimes do this in the cool of the larder overnight, as the slower it rises the better the bread. But it always does rise, don't panic!

8. When risen, cook in a moderate oven 190C/375F/Gas mark 5 for about 40 minutes. In my 2 oven Aga, the bottom oven is too cool and the top too hot, unless I use the cool shelf above the bread, to deflect the heat.

9. Turn out, replace in the oven upside down for a further 5 minutes.
Cool on a wire rack.

With home made marmalade, this makes the best breakfast EVER.

. . . and if you want a delicious home made marmalade see Penelope Keith's recipe on page 201.

Michael Caines MBE
CHEF AND RESTAURATEUR

Chocolate Fudge Cake

225g plain dark chocolate
225g unsalted butter
345g caster sugar
6 eggs, separated into yolks and whites
120g ground almonds
145g soft white breadcrumbs
30g plain flour
1 tsp vanilla essence

Icing:
85g cocoa powder
255g icing sugar
130g butter
170g caster sugar
6 tablespoons water
1 round tin – 26cm in diameter

1. Firstly, preheat the oven to 160C /325F/Gas mark 3.
2. To make the cake, melt the chocolate in a double boiler, or in a bowl placed over a pan of boiling water.
3. In a separate bowl, cream together the butter and the sugar until white and soft.
4. Add the egg yolks gradually, one by one, then add the almonds and beat them in.
5. After this, gently fold in the chocolate with a spoon, then add the bread crumbs, flour and vanilla essence and mix together.
6. In a separate bowl, beat the egg whites, along with a pinch of sugar, until stiff – but do not over beat.
7. Fold the egg whites into the cake mixture and then pour the mixture into your buttered cake tin (lined with paper).
8. Place in the oven and cook for 1 hour.
During this time make the icing:
9. Place the cocoa powder and the icing sugar in a mixing bowl.
10. Warm together the butter, sugar and water until dissolved.
11. Add the liquid into the dry mixture and mix together for a thick but 'pourable' consistency.
12. Once the cake has cooked and cooled, pour over the cake. Enjoy!

Stephen Fry
ACTOR AND TV PERSONALITY

Honey Buns

75g caster sugar
1 teaspoon soft dark sugar
Pinch salt
90g self-raising flour
2 eggs
1 teaspoon baking powder
90g melted butter, cooled
1 tablespoon honey

1. Whisk together the eggs and sugars.
2. Fold in the sifted flour, baking powder and salt.
3. Leave the mixture to rest for 30 minutes.
4. Stir in the melted butter and honey.
5. Bake in paper cases for approx 25 minutes at 180C/350F/Gas mark 4

'The rations now arriv'd, each took his share, And eagerly devour'd the scanty Fare; And scanty Fare it was, consisting chief Of flinty Biscuits, tough and stinking beef...'
The Military Adventures of Johnny Newcome

Hannah Gordon
ACTRESS

Malt Loaf

This is a very good recipe for children and also for me, because it's so easy!

2 cups of self-raising flour
1 cup of dark brown sugar
1 cup of raisins
1 cup of warmed milk
1 tablespoon of black treacle
A pinch of salt

One cup = 250ml or 8 fl oz

1. In a large bowl, sieve the flour and the salt, then add the sugar and the raisins.
2. Dissolve the treacle in the warmed milk and add this to the bowl.
3. Stir everything together and pour the mixture into a greased loaf tin.
4. Bake in the oven for 1 hour at 180C/350F/Gas mark 4.
5. After baking, leave the loaf in the tin for 2-3 minutes and then turn out on to a rack to cool.

Slice and butter.

'One of the very nicest things about life is the way we must regularly stop whatever it is we are doing and devote our attention to eating.'
Luciano Pavarotti and William Wright, Pavarotti, My Own Story

---

Nicholas Hoult

ACTOR

My Nan's Lemon Drizzle Cake

175g softened butter
275g caster sugar
Finely grated zest of 2 lemons
3 large eggs
225g self-raising flour
100ml lemon juice

1. Preheat the oven to 180C/350F/Gas Mark 4. Line the cake tin with baking paper.
2. Put butter, 175g caster sugar and lemon zest in bowl.
3. Beat until light and fluffy. Use an electric whisk or beat by hand if muscular.
4. Add eggs, one at a time, beat them in each time with a tablespoon of flour.
5. Fold in the rest of the flour and put in cake tin.
6. Bake in the oven for 45 minutes, until well risen and springy in the middle.
7. Meanwhile, place the rest of the sugar and lemon juice in a bowl and stir.
8. When the cake is cooked, leave in the tin and pierce all over.
9. Slowly drizzle the lemon mixture on the top so that it soaks into the cake. It should set to a lovely crunchy crust on the top.

Happy eating!

SERVES 12 (or 4 in the Hoult household)

Dorothy Hughes
CHELSEA PENSIONER
Welsh Cakes

In 2009, Dorothy made history by being one of the first two ladies to be admitted to the Royal Hospital since its foundation in 1682. Dorothy has already arranged for her legendary Welsh Cakes to be cooked for the Pensioners.

8 oz self raising flour
4 oz butter
3 oz castor sugar
1 teaspoon baking powder
¼ teaspoon cinnamon
3 oz sultanas
1 oz mixed peel
1 teaspoon lemon juice
1 large egg
Small quantity of milk if mix is too dry
Small amount of flour for rolling out mixture

1. Put flour, butter, sugar, baking powder and cinnamon into food mixer and mix well.
2. Add the beaten egg with the lemon juice.
3. Mix until it forms a cake-like consistency.
4. Pulse in the fruit.
5. Turn out onto a lightly-floured pastry board and roll out to ½ inch thickness.
6. Cut into 2½ inch circles.
7. Put a lightly greased griddle or very heavy frying pan over a very low heat.
8. Brown the cakes on one side for about 2 minutes then turn them over and repeat the process.
9. Place on a wire try to cool then dust with icing sugar.

This quantity makes about 20 cakes and you can store them for 1–2 weeks.

P. D. James OBE

AUTHORESS

Chocolate Buns

I have great affection for this recipe because when my children were young during the war I would make these chocolate buns as a treat for Sunday tea. They normally ate the first buns straight from the oven but in the war, of course, I couldn't include the chocolate.

6 oz plain flour
1 oz cocoa powder
1 tsp baking powder
½ tsp bicarbonate of soda
6oz plain chocolate broken into small chunks
2 eggs, beaten
4 oz soft brown sugar
4 oz soft butter

Preheat oven to 200C/400F/Gas mark 6
Butter 10 muffin/patty tins

1. Using a wooden spoon, cream together sugar and butter, then add the eggs gradually and beat in hard.
2. Combine flour, cocoa powder, baking powder and bicarbonate of soda, and sift all together.
3. Slowly fold into the mixture using a spatula. Finally mix in the chunks of chocolate.
4. Generously fill the patty tins – the mixture should be quite stiff.
5. Cook for 20 minutes until the buns have risen, then leave in tin for another 15 minutes (otherwise the buns will disintegrate).
6. Remove and place on a wire rack to cool – ready for Sunday tea!

MAKES 10 BUNS

Penelope Keith CBE
ACTRESS

Chunky Orange Marmalade

4 lbs Seville oranges
2 sweet oranges
2 lemons
6 pints water
6 lbs sugar

1. Wash fruit thoroughly.
2. Put in large pan with water and simmer slowly until tender enough to pierce easily with a fork. This takes approximately one hour.
3. Take off heat and allow to cool.
4. Remove the fruit, but leave the water in the pan.
5. Cut fruit in half and remove pips and pith, then shred and slice the skin, not too fine or the marmalade will not be chunky.
6. Return the cut-up fruit to the pan with the water in which the oranges were cooked, stir in the sugar and bring to the boil.
7. Simmer moderately fast until a little of the marmalade will set when tested.
8. Pot whilst hot.

The ideal accompaniment to Emma Bridgewater's Home Made Bread (page 192).

'I got the blues thinking of the future, so I left off and made some marmalade. It's amazing how it cheers one up to shred oranges and scrub the floor.'
D H Lawrence

Nigella Lawson
CHEF

Snow-flecked Brownies

375g best quality dark chocolate
375g unsalted butter at room temperature at least
1 tablespoon real vanilla extract
6 eggs
350g sugar
1 teaspoon salt
225g plain flour
250g white chocolate buttons, preferably Montgomery Moore,
    or just chop same amount of good white chocolate

Tin measuring approx 33cm x 23cm x 5.5cm

Preheat the oven to 180C/350F/ Gas mark 4
1. Line your brownie pan base and sides.
2. Melt the butter and dark chocolate together in a large heavy based pan.
3. In a bowl or wide mouthed large measuring jug, beat the eggs with the sugar and vanilla.
4. Measure the flour into another bowl and add the salt.
5. When the chocolate mixture has melted let it cool a bit before beating in the eggs and sugar, and then the flour.
6. Finally fold in the white chocolate buttons. Beat to combine smoothly and then scrape out the saucepan into the lined pan. Bake for about 25 minutes.
7. The brownies are ready when the top is dried to a paler brown speckle but the middle is dark and dense and gooey still; remember that they will continue to cook as they cool.

Feast by Nigella Lawson (Chatto and Windus 2004) © Nigella Lawson 2004

Joanna Lumley OBE
ACTRESS

Sephardic Orange Cake

I'm rather a wretched cook, but a keen collector of recipes and this one I can wholeheartedly recommend.

2 oranges, preferably organic
6 eggs, free range
225g ground almonds
1 teaspoon baking powder
175g castor sugar

1. Cover the oranges with water in a pan and bring to the boil. Simmer for an hour.   Drain, de-pip and process until you have a purée.
2. Line a 20 cm round cake tin.
3. Whisk eggs and sugar in mixer until meringue-like, then fold in other ingredients and mix well.
4. Pour into tin and bake for 50–60 minutes at 190C/375F/Gas mark 5.

Needless to say it is rather good as a pudding with a blob of cream or Greek yoghurt on top

SERVES 8

'If a man be sensible and one fine morning, while he is lying in bed, count at the tips of his fingers how many things in this life truly will give him enjoyment, invariably he will find food is the first one.'
Lin Yutang

Claire Macdonald
CHEF AND HOTELIER

Dark Chocolate and Ginger Squares

8 oz/225g butter, cut into bits

8 oz/225g dark chocolate broken into bits

2 large egg yolks

8 oz/225g ginger biscuits, crushed in a thick polythene bag, using a rolling pin

3 tablespoons ginger wine e.g. Crabbie's

8 pieces of stem ginger, drained of its syrup and the ginger diced neatly and finely

4 oz/120g toasted pistachio nuts, bashed, but not to fine crumbs, just broken up

1. Base line a square or oblong tin measuring about 12" by 10" (20 by 24 cm) with baking parchment.

2. Put the bashed and crumb-like ginger biscuits into a mixing bowl. Mix the 3 tablespoons of ginger wine thoroughly through the biscuits crumbs.

3. Melt together the chocolate and butter, over a gentle heat in a heavy based saucepan. Stir together to give a thick, glossy, chocolate cream.

4. Beat the egg yolks into the hot chocolate and butter mixture - the heat will cook the yolks.

5. Mix the ginger biscuit crumbs and the pistachio nuts into the chocolate mixture, mixing as thoroughly as you can.

6. Scrape this mixture into the prepared tin and smooth even. Leave to set.

7. Mark and cut into squares before it is too cold, this is easier when it isn't too brittle.

MAKES ABOUT 16

Charlie Mayfield

CHAIRMAN JOHN LEWIS PARTNERSHIP

Banana Bread

This is a family favourite:

¼ cup (2½ oz) butter or margarine (melted)
2 eggs
1 cup (8 oz) sugar
⅛ teaspoon salt
1½ cups (12 oz) plain flour
1 teaspoon bicarbonate of soda
3 large or 4 small ripe bananas

1. In a bowl mix all the dry ingredients together.
2. In a separate bowl lightly beat the eggs with a fork, add the melted butter/margarine and then add it all to the dry ingredients and stir.
3. Mash the bananas and fold them into the mixture until well blended.
4. Pour mixture into greased or lined loaf tin.
5. Bake at 160C/325F/Gas mark 3 for one hour.
6. Test with skewer or toothpick. The cake is ready when the skewer comes out clean.
7. Turn cake out onto a wire rack to cool.

Tip:
If the final mixture is stiff you can loosen it by adding a dash of milk.

'All sorrows are less with bread.'
Don Quixote

206

Michel Roux

CHEF AND RESTAURATEUR

Roux's Chelsea Buns

This bun was initially associated with the Bun House in Chelsea in the early 18th century, being baked first in the cellars along the Pimlico Road, under the premises now used by furniture designer David Linley. The Bun House was patronised by the royal family and also by visitors to the Royal Hospital.

500g strong bread flour
75g caster sugar
1 tsp salt
75g butter
35g yeast
250ml milk, tepid
1 egg
Grated zest of ½ lemon
50g sultanas
50g melted butter
½ tbsp cinnamon
½ tbsp icing sugar

1. Sift the flour, sugar and salt together, then gently rub in the butter. Dissolve the yeast in the tepid milk and add the egg. Gradually mix this with the flour until you have a dough texture – dust the work surface with extra flour to avoid it sticking.
2. Place the dough in a bowl, cover and leave to prove until it has doubled in size.
3. Knock the dough back and roll out into a rectangle measuring about 20cm x 40cm. Brush with the melted butter and sprinkle with the sultanas and lemon zest. Mix together the cinnamon and icing sugar and sprinkle over the dough. Roll up the dough, starting from the longest edge, and cut the roll into about 15 pieces.
4. Place the buns on a non-stick baking tray, making sure they are not too close together. Leave to rise for 15–20 minutes.
5. Cook in a hot oven 210C/425F/Gas mark 7 for 15 minutes. The buns should be golden-brown, moist and all stuck together. Leave to cool on a wire rack before separating.

MAKES 15 BUNS

A Life in the Kitchen by Michel Roux (Weidenfeld & Nicolson, The Orion Publishing Group 2009) © Michel Roux 2009.

Phil Vickery

CHEF

Parkin

This is my mum's recipe and I'm assured by my dad that it's very good indeed. I can't stand ground ginger so unfortunately it's out for me. Lancashire and Yorkshire both have recipes for Parkin; I'm not telling you which side of the Pennines this came from.

This makes 1 loaf approximately 8" x 10"

225g plain soft flour
225g unrefined brown castor sugar
280g black treacle
225g oatmeal
1 level tsp ground ginger
2 pinches salt
180g unsalted butter
1 level tsp bicarbonate of soda
1 level tsp mixed spice

Set the oven to 180C/350F/ Gas mark 4

1. Sift the flour, salt, ginger and mixed spice together.
2. Add the oatmeal and stir well.
3. Melt the treacle, sugar and butter together until nice and runny.
4. Dissolve the bicarbonate of soda in the milk.
5. Pour the melted butter mixture into the dry ingredients and add the milk and bicarb too.
6. Carefully stir together and pour into the prepared baking tray.
7. Cook in the pre-heated oven until well risen and firm, about 45 minutes.
8. Cool and cut into large squares.

I like to serve this with either a cup of strong tea, or warm with syrup custard.

And finally...

General the Lord Walker GCB CMG CBE DL
CHIEF OF THE DEFENCE STAFF 2003-2006, GOVERNOR ROYAL HOSPITAL CHELSEA
Leather Bottle Wine

This recipe came from my grandmother and is powerful stuff which needs to be drunk in moderation! As a young and impecunious officer it was the saving grace at a number of ad-hoc gatherings and, although we never invited any *sommeliers*, we were never short of thirsty takers.

3 gallons water
8 lbs granulated sugar
5 lbs short grain rice
3 lbs sultanas
4 oranges
1 oz Allison's dried yeast

1. Boil the water.
2. Place sugar in a container (a plastic dustbin is a good choice), pour the boiling water over it and stir until dissolved.
3. When the liquid is luke-warm, add the rice, sultanas and sliced oranges.
4. Mix the yeast with a little warm liquid to which has been added one teaspoon of sugar and stir into the mixture.
5. Keep the container at 65° to 85° F stirring once a day (the airing cupboard is a good place).
6. Rack into demijohns - it will be cloudy to start with but will clear in a few days and may then be decanted ready for drinking.

The Christmas Cheese Ceremony
AT THE ROYAL HOSPITAL CHELSEA

The annual Christmas Cheese Ceremony at the Royal Hospital Chelsea dates back to 1959, when the members of the English Dairy Council offered to present each Chelsea Pensioner with a pound of cheese to sustain them over the Christmas period.

Cheese has always formed a core part of the Pensioners' diet. The original order, dated 1692 and laying down 'the nature and charge of the diet of the persons to be lodged at the Royal Hospital Chelsea', stipulated ½ pound of cheese a day for each man, to be served with bread and ale for supper. The first cheesemonger to supply cheese in the 1690s, sourced originally from Worcestershire and later from Gloucestershire, charged just 3d per pound.

Today the Dairy Council continues to organise this festive occasion in early December. Farmers from all over the country donate their products to create a mouth-watering display of British cheeses from all over the United Kingdom. In recent years, contributions have included Cornish Yarg from the south-west; Arran Blue from the Isle of Arran in Scotland; Black Bomber, Green Thunder and Red Devil from Snowdonia in Wales; not to mention cheddars from Dorset, Gloucestershire and Cheshire; and stiltons galore. The party traditionally concludes with one of the oldest Pensioners ceremonially cutting the largest cheese with an officer's sword, followed by much hearty singing of a song known as The Quartermaster's Stores, to the accompaniment of a military band:

There was cheese, cheese, wafting on the breeze,
In the Stores, in the Stores.
There was jam, jam, mixed up with the ham,
In the Quartermaster's Stores.

Chorus
My eyes are dim, I cannot see
I have not brought my specs with me
I have not brought my specs with me.

There was meat, meat. Meat you couldn't eat,
In the Stores, in the Stores.
There were eggs, eggs, nearly growing legs,
In the Quartermaster's Stores.

Chorus

There was bread, bread. Just like lumps of lead,
In the Stores, in the Stores.
There were buns, buns, bullets for the guns,
In the Quartermaster's Stores.

Chorus

There were mice, mice, eating all the rice,
In the Stores, in the Stores.
There were rats, rats, big as blooming cats,
In the Quartermaster's Stores.

Chorus

There was beer, beer, beer you can't get near,
In the Stores, in the Stores.
There was rum, rum, just for the General's tum,
In the Quartermaster's Stores.

Chorus

213

The Cake Ceremony

Every year since 1950 a large Christmas Cake has been presented to the Royal Hospital by the Returned Sailors', Soldiers' and Airmens' Imperial League of Australia. The League does this in remembrance of the 59,259 losses to the Australian Armed Forces in World War I and the 30,552 losses in World War II. During the ceremony in the Great Hall a Chelsea Pensioner cuts the huge cake with a sword, and then, with the accompanying military band, all sing *Advance Australia Fair, Waltzing Matilda* and *Auld Lang Syne*.

Stirring the Christmas Pudding

In early December, near to the last Sunday before Advent, which is called *Stir Up Sunday*, the community of the Royal Hospital meets in the Great Hall to mix the ingredients that will make 75 puddings, each weighing 500g. These will supply the Chelsea Pensioners during the festive season. The atmosphere is of a large family gathering, with staff and Chelsea Pensioners taking turns to add an ingredient to the mixture in a large 'canvas' bath, and then stir it in with a giant wooden spoon. The atmosphere is enhanced by a lively military band and refreshments followed by lusty communal singing of the first Christmas carols of the season.

ROYAL HOSPITAL CHELSEA

Traditional Christmas Pudding

FOR 75 X 500GM PUDDINGS	INGREDIENTS	FAMILY SIZE PUDDING
2.8kg	Flour	57gm
5.4kg	Butchers Rusk	85gm
4.95kg	Chopped Suet	113gm
4.75kg	Demerara Sugar	85mg
4.95kg	Currants	113gm
4.95kg	Sultanas	113gm
4.75kg	Stoneless Raisins	85gm
1,7kg	Candied Mixed Peel	40gm
1.7kg	Glace Cherries	40gm
0.30kg	Ground Almonds	7gm
0.30kg	Flaked Almonds	7gm
16 Nos.	Oranges (Grated Zest only)	1 No.
5 Nos.	Lemons (Grated Zest only)	1 Small
4.75kg	Eating Apples (Cored, Peeled & Sliced)	1 Small
168gm	Mixed Spice	7gm
168gm	Ginger (Powdered)	7gm
70 Nos.	Eggs	2 No.
7.5 Pints	Old Ale	0.28 lt.
14 Pints	Guinness	0.28 lt.
2 Bottles	Rum	1 tot
2 Bottles	Brandy	1 tot
2 Bottles	Sherry	1 tot
2 Bottles	Port	1 tot

Method:

1. Wash all the fruit and mix it together with all the dry ingredients.
2. Make a bay in the centre and into this pour all the liquids and the eggs.
3. Stir the whole mix thoroughly and allow to stand for 24 hours.
4. Divide the mixture into well greased 2lb and 1lb pudding basins and cover.
5. Steam or boil for a minimum of 4 hours.
6. When cold, remove the cover and wrap in greaseproof paper and a clean cloth. Tie with cord.
7. Store until required.
8. Boil for a further 2 ½ hours, serve with Brandy Sauce, Brandy Butter or Thick Double Cream.

Founder's Day Feasts at the Royal Hospital Chelsea

Founder's Day, or Oak Apple Day, has been celebrated annually without a break since the opening of the Royal Hospital in 1692. Although now held in early June (to avoid clashing with the Chelsea Flower Show), it formerly took place on 29 May every year to commemorate both the birthday of the founder, King Charles II, and the date of his restoration to the monarchy in 1660.

In the eighteenth century the In-Pensioners were served with a double quantity of food and beer on Founder's Day. By 1810 the Hospital's Commissioners were spending £50 a year on provisions to celebrate Oak Apple Day and the reigning monarch's birthday, with a similar sum for alcoholic refreshments. In 1806 the drinks served at the Governor's Table during the Founder's Day feast included ale, beer, cider, claret, madeira, port, porter, sherry, and spirits. Not surprisingly, these events became something of a social occasion, and in 1783 the author and lawyer James Boswell secured his first invitation to attend the special dinner on 29 May, which began at 3 p.m.:

Sir George Howard was very courteous to me during the whole repast, and after it was over asked me to dine there every anniversary as long as he was Governor.

I sat between Mr. [Edmund] Burke and Dr. Mounsey, who in his eighty-ninth year was quite entire in his mind. … He told me brandy was very pernicious to the Stomack. … We had an excellent dinner, and a great deal of good wines. I drank liberally, was in high spirits and very happy in my talk …

In spite of his great age, Dr Messenger Mounsey was serving as Physician at the Royal Hospital at this time. Boswell described him as 'a fellow who swore and talked bawdy'. He also had a strange sense of humour: in his will he bequeathed an old velvet coat to one friend, and the buttons on it to another.

Boswell continued to attend the annual feasts until 29 May 1790, when he wrote a lengthy description of what appears to have been his last visit to the event:

It was an excellent dinner, as usual, and I drank of all the liquors: Cold drink, small beer, ale, porter, cyder, Madeira, sherry, old hock, port, Claret. I was in good spirits at the Festival, talked well… and we circulated the glass a long time. … I was much intoxicated, and I suppose talked nonsense. Very irregular this; but I thought the festival an excuse.

The following day, the first entry in Boswell's diary reads: 'Awaked somewhat feverish.'

216

'Biscuits appear to have arrived in 3 states: hard and jaw-breaking, alive with maggots or crushed to crumbs and mouldered to dust. In November 1813 each man was given a biscuit nearly an inch thick and requiring a hammer to break it. Lieutenant Wyndham Maddam stuffed one into the breast pocket of his jacket – 'early in the day the biscuit was shattered to pieces and saved his life.'
Life in Wellington's Army (1972) Anthony Brett-James

The Chelsea Pensioners' Meals in 1692

By the time the Royal Hospital Chelsea admitted its first residents in 1692, the catering arrangements had been carefully planned. Each pensioner was allowed 12 oz. of meat a day, except on Fridays, when a similar portion of fish was provided. In addition they had two loaves of bread, ½ lb. of cheese, two quarts of beer, and an unspecified quantity of oatmeal and vegetables. The Steward supervised the supply of all provisions, and was expected to 'take care that the gardeners dry herbs proper and sufficient for the Porridge in the Winter Season.'

The Master Cook was given strict instructions to check on the quality of the food provided, and precise details on how and when it was to be served:

You are every day betweene Eleven and Twelve a Clock, when the Drum beats, to begin to Dish the said Meat, Delivering out first the Dishes for the Five Tables in the Officers Hall, next those for the Sixteen Tables below the Steppe in the Great Hall, Next those for the Governours Table upon the Steppe, And lastly those for the Housekeepers Hall and the Servants Hall, which are not to be served till one a Clock.

Meals were served under the supervision of the Master Butler, who was also paid £15 a year for supplying mustard. In addition to looking after all the cloths, plate and pewter, he was instructed to:

… take care the Bakers lay the Bread, and that the Butter is brought upon the proper days, and the Mustard upon the Beef days; to receive the Beer from the

Brewer, to superintend the drawing of it, and to take care that it is not drawn lower than it runs fine; to receive the Cheese and Butter sent for the use of the Hospital, and cut the same according to the several allowances of the House; if not good to acquaint the Comptroller and Steward therewith; to see that the Quart Pots are kept sweet and clean, and to keep an account of the beer, cheese and butter.

The Usher of the Hall – who swept up, tended fires, cleared tables, and extinguished candles – was also told … not to suffer strangers to come into the [Great] Hall when the Pensioners are at dinner, but if they desire to see them eat to admit them in the Gallery; to keep Dogs out and not to suffer Tobacco to be taken in; to make a Fire in the middle of the Hall when directed, taking care to light it half an hour before Dinner and Supper, and put it out and carry the ashes away when Supper is done.

Visiting the Great Hall at mealtimes seems to have become a popular event for members of the public, and in 1705 a Westminster schoolmaster, who was living in Chelsea, recorded that the pensioners 'Dine and Sup every Day in the Hall in great Order, having a plentiful Allowance.'

'The pensioners sat on benches attached to the sixteen tables with iron bars and the tables were covered with cloths. These tablecloths would – as was the custom – have reached to the floor and doubled up as napkins.'
Royal Hospital Book of Instructions 1692

COME AND VISIT THE CHELSEA PENSIONERS AND FIND OUT HOW A DONATION OR A GIFT IN YOUR WILL CAN HELP MAINTAIN THEIR HOME

The Royal Hospital Chelsea has been looking after old and infirm veteran soldiers for well over three centuries since it was first occupied in 1692. Our duty today is to make sure it can continue doing so for the next Century and beyond, so that it remains as a living testament to the sacrifice of successive generations of soldiers in the service of their Nation.

To do this we have embarked on a major development programme to make the Royal Hospital fit for purpose in the 21st Century and beyond. Already we have raised enough money to have the new Margaret Thatcher Infirmary built, which today stands handsomely alongside the original Wren and Soane buildings. Moreover, it was built to budget and on time, an achievement of which we are very proud. The Infirmary has also enabled us to offer interim accommodation to

our first Ladies, who joined us as Chelsea Pensioners in March 2009.

The next step is to modernise the historic Long Wards, in which the majority of Chelsea Pensioners live in conditions Wren would instantly recognise were he to return. Once that has been completed, we intend progressively to build an endowment to guarantee the long-term survival of this important and much loved national institution.

Very appropriately, the Government provides us with a considerable grant-in-aid to help with our day-to-day running costs. But the Royal Hospital is not Government owned, and we rely on the generosity of our friends and support from the public to fund capital projects, together with making the best possible use of our own assets.

We believe that military service is unique in the demands that it places on individuals, and that in return the Government and the Nation have a duty towards those who are prepared to make the ultimate sacrifice. Indeed, this is the basis of the Military Covenant, that essential and unbreakable bond between those who serve in the Armed Forces, the Government, which employs them, and the people whose freedom they defend.

We are very grateful to you for playing your part in this by giving us your support; and we hope you will remain a friend and supporter of the Royal Hospital in future.

THE CHELSEA PENSIONERS' *Appeal*

THANK YOU
FOR YOUR SUPPORT

THE CHELSEA PENSIONERS' *Appeal*

Lance Corporal Michael Faulkner
(recently wounded on operations)
could be eligible to become a
Chelsea Pensioner in 2049

For more information about preparing to leave a legacy or making a gift please contact

Development Department
e-mail: Legacy.gifts@chelsea-pensioners.org.uk
Tel: 0207 881 5537

The Royal Hospital Chelsea likes to acknowledge supporters in the timeless fabric of our unique environment

The Chelsea Pensioners Appeal
Registered in England Charity Number: 1076414

Contributors